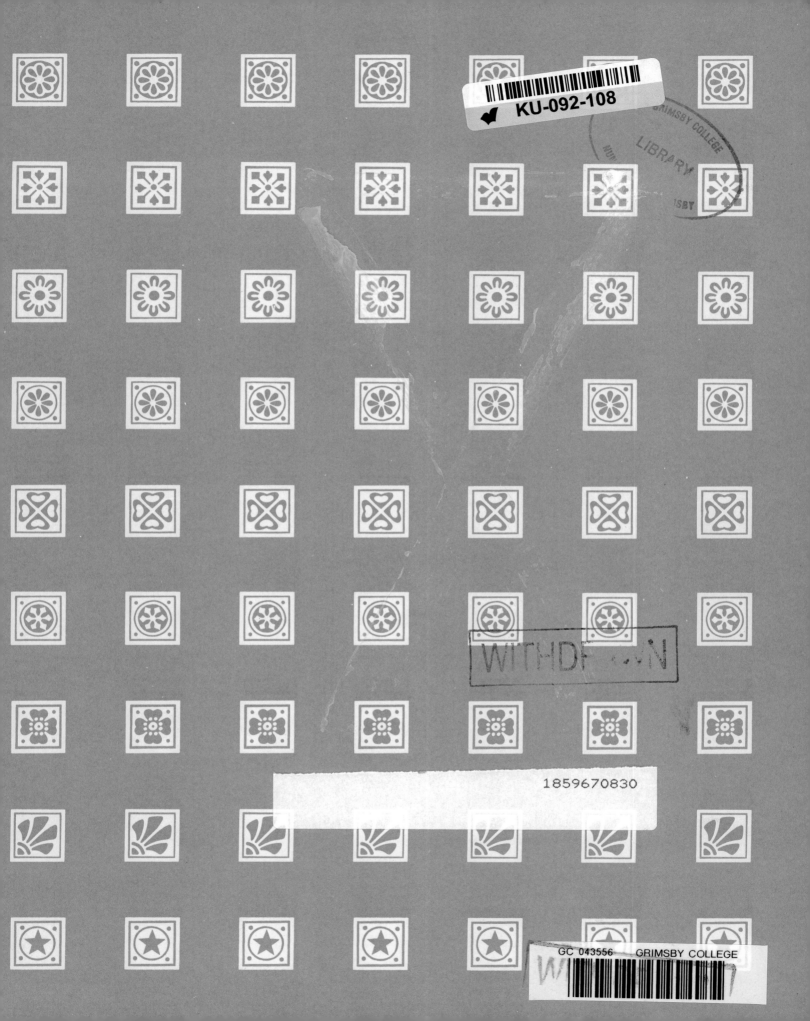

FRAME
W·O·R·K·S

FRAME
W·O·R·K·S

JULIET BAWDEN

LORENZ BOOKS
LONDON · NEW YORK · SYDNEY · BATH

For Tarja Kurhela for all your help over the last year. I could not have managed without you!

Publisher's Note

Crafts and hobbies are great fun to learn and can fill many rewarding hours of leisure time, but some general points should be remembered for safety and care of the environment.

■ Always use non-toxic materials, for example paints, glues and varnishes. If this is not possible, always use materials in a well-ventilated area and always follow the manufacturer's instructions.

■ Craft knives, needles, scissors and all sharp instruments should be used with care. Always use a cutting board or mat to avoid damage to household surfaces (it is also safer to cut on to a firm, non-slip surface).

■ Protect surfaces from paint, glue and varnish splashes by laying down old newspapers, plastic sheeting or an old sheet.

This edition first published by Lorenz Books

Lorenz Books is an imprint of
Anness Publishing Limited
1 Boundary Row
London SE1 8HP

ISBN 1 85967 083 0

A CIP catalog record for this book is available from the British Library

Distributed in Australia by Reed Editions

Typeset by MC Typeset Limited

Printed and bound in Hong Kong

Publisher: Joanna Lorenz
Project Editors: Emma Wish and Judith Simons
Designer: Kit Johnson
Special Photography: Steve Tanner
Step-by-Step Photography: Lucy Tizard
Stylist: Gillie Spargo
Illustrator: Anna Koska

CONTENTS

INTRODUCTION

THIS BOOK IS ABOUT MAKING DECORATIVE FRAMES. IT IS NOT THE USUAL DO-IT-YOURSELF BOOK ABOUT MAKING MOUNTS (MATS) AND THE MERITS OF DIFFERENT MOULDINGS – ALTHOUGH THE BASIC PRINCIPLES AND TECHNIQUES OF MOUNTING AND FRAMING ARE CLEARLY EXPLAINED. IT IS A BOOK WHICH ENCOMPASSES MUCH MORE THAN THE BASIC WAYS OF SURROUNDING A PICTURE OR A MIRROR.

The core of the book is a large project section covering a wide range of techniques, to enable you to choose the right sort of frame for your art work. You can learn how to construct frames out of many different materials, including paper, cardboard, papier-mâché, salt dough and natural materials. There are fabric frames, decorated by techniques including painting, hand-hooking and cross-stitching. For those who like something a little more zany, there are novelty frames and there is a chapter on frames suitable for children.

Many of the frames shown in the photographs are surrounding mirrors; mirrors are a particularly effective way of showing off a spectacular frame because they don't compete with the frame, as an image might. But nearly all the frames are just as suitable for images as mirrors, so you can choose whichever you prefer.

As well as how to make new frames, this volume also covers methods of decorating and revamping existing frames. We show how you can carry out simple repairs to damaged plaster,

wooden, papier-mâché and gilt frames. All techniques are illustrated with clear step-by-step photographs. As styles of pictures and paintings have changed over the years, so have the frames in which they are mounted: sometimes the frame is of little importance; at other times it is more so. A picture with a well chosen mount (mat) and frame is like a well wrapped present. It is with this thought in mind that we have included a section on different ways of hanging pictures.

As you will see throughout this book, frames can be an art-form in their own right. They do not have to be confined to a supporting rôle to a work of art: they are attractive, decorative objects on their own. Frames can be used to surround much-loved items. For example, hang a hat on the wall and surround it by a frame. Hang your jewellery in the centre of a frame decorated with fake jewels. Surround a skeletal leaf with pieces of smooth driftwood. A collection of precious items can be displayed in a box frame that is divided into compartments.

This book is a gallery of inspirational frames made by many different artists. Many different crafts are included in this book, most of which need very little specialist equipment and therefore are inexpensive to do. Most of the ideas can be achieved in an evening or less, although in the case of something such as salt dough there will inevitably be longish intervals of waiting time.

Once you start making frames, you may find you cannot stop! They are great decorative features and make good presents.

Above: pieces of driftwood have been put together in a simple construction to surround a mirror. The addition of the seagull gives the frame a strong seashore feel.

Opposite: a punched tin frame decorated with Folk Art-style motifs.

FRAMING TECHNIQUES

THIS IS NOT A CONVENTIONAL BOOK ABOUT FRAMING, HOWEVER, THIS CHAPTER COVERS ALL THE TECHNIQUES AND EQUIPMENT NECESSARY TO ENABLE YOU TO MAKE A BASIC WOODEN FRAME AND MOUNT. FOLLOW THE STEP-BY-STEP PHOTOGRAPHS FOR MAKING MOUNTS, FRAMES, CUTTING GLASS AND FINISHING OFF, AS WELL AS THE SUGGESTIONS FOR DECORATING MOUNTS. IF YOU HAVE AN OLD FRAME WHICH NEEDS SOME ATTENTION, THIS CHAPTER SHOWS YOU HOW TO CARRY OUT SIMPLE REPAIRS. IF YOU ARE FED UP WITH THE SHAPE OF A FRAME, READ THE SECTION ON ADAPTING FRAMES FOR IDEAS ON HOW TO ALTER THE BASIC SHAPE. BE INSPIRED BY OUR SUGGESTIONS FOR HANGING FRAMES – SIMPLE WAYS OF MAKING YOUR FRAME A SPECIAL FEATURE.

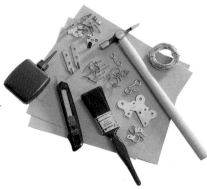

CHOOSING FRAMES

Although it is somewhat of a cliché, there is a saying amongst framers that the greater the merit or value of the picture, the more restrained the frame should be. A poor picture might be improved dramatically by surrounding it with the right frame. A more significant work needs to be handled with sensitivity, so that it is not overwhelmed by the frame. When choosing a frame, then, you need to consider both the picture and the mount (mat) together. The aim is to achieve a perfect balance: a visual harmony. For example, oil paintings tend to be heavily textured, with intense colours, and give an impression of weight; they need a bold frame, perhaps heavy and chunky or ornate and gilded. A water-colour is lighter in appearance and needs a lighter-weight and lighter-coloured frame if it is not to be overpowered.

Pots of waxy cream are used for covering scratches and cracks in moulding. The crayons are for filling nail holes. Both come in a range of colours so you can match your moulding.

Because the mount is next to the picture, this must also be taken into account when framing. A dark mount creates a strong band of colour that can dominate a picture, so it is probably better to make a dark mount narrower than is usual.

When choosing the right frame, scale has an important part to play. Small pictures, particularly oils, can look completely lost if they are placed in a small frame. The answer is to place them in a frame proportionately wider than one would use for a larger painting. The frame will draw the viewer's eye towards it and on into the picture. Small water-colours can be treated in the same way, but you must take care with the colour of the frame, to ensure it does not overwhelm the painting within.

When buying a frame, if possible take the piece of work it is to surround – whether it be a print, poster, painting or piece of needlework – with you. If you do this, you can make sure the frame and image suit one another. If you find the right frame but don't like the mount, or it doesn't have a mount, make a new one (see pages 14–15).

There are two main types of moulding: framer's moulding and builder's moulding. The difference between them is that builder's moulding does not come with a rebate (rabbet) a right-angled notch under the frame that allows the picture, mount (mat) and glass to fit neatly into place without falling out of the frame. Builder's moulding is primarily used for trimming doors, windows, skirtings and other interior finishes. Framer's moulding is more expensive, but for a beginner it is the easiest type of moulding to use. If you have to use builder's moulding, you can add a narrow piece of wood behind the moulding to create a false rebate. The heavier the frame, the wider the rebate will need to be to support the weight of the frame. Framer's moulding is available in a number of widths, types and finishes. A good framing shop will carry a variety of styles; remember that you can always add your own finish.

There are four main categories of frame mouldings. The *swept frame* has a high outside edge and sweeps down in a curve to the sight (the part near the picture) edge. The opposite shape to this is the *reverse profile frame*; this shape has been popular since the sixteenth century. The highest part of the moulding is near to the picture and it has the effect of thrusting the picture forward. The *border* or *casseta* type of moulding combines a flat border with a raised, curved profile. The *flat-faced* frame type is perhaps the most common. These borders can be decorated in many ways or left plain.

If you don't wish to decorate your own moulding, there is a wide variety of ready-made finishes from which to choose: reproduction antique; period-style; marbled; vinegar-grained; crackled; gold-leaf; limed and lacquered are just a few available in a number of different widths and colours. Great care should be taken when using pre-decorated mouldings, as many have fragile finishes or come highly glossed in a way that can easily be damaged.

Wooden frames do not have to be treated: the wood itself may be very beautiful in its natural state, for example a walnut, cherry or maple wood looks beautiful on its own. There are dyes, waxes and stains available for the more mundane softwoods such as pine.

Opposite: a selection of mouldings showing a variety of shapes and colours available.

EQUIPMENT

1 Mitre Saw Used for cutting moulding at accurate angles. This type has a range of pre-set angles and an integral saw.

2 Wood Glue Strong adhesive for gluing mitre joints together.

3 Picture Wire Strong multistranded copper wire used for hanging frames.

4 Panel Pins For pinning frames and fixing backing board in to position.

5 Screw-Eyes These are screwed in to the back of the frame, and the picture wire is attached to them.

6 Hand Drill For drilling pins or nails in to the frame to secure the moulding.

7 Tack Hammer For hammering panel pins and nails.

8 Hacksaw For cutting hardboard.

9 Wire Cutters Used to remove the heads from nails and for cutting picture wire.

10 Pliers For bending wire and removing old nails and panel pins.

11 Nail Punch For recessing nails prior to filling.

12 Bradawl (Awl) Used to make guide holes for nails and screws.

13 Self-healing Cutting Mat For cutting on when using a craft knife.

14 Metal Carpenter's Square For marking and cutting accurate right angles.

15 Pencil For marking measurements on mounts (mats) and moulding.

16 Ruler For accurate measuring.

17 Metal Rule To use as a guide when cutting straight lines with a craft knife or mount (mat) cutter.

18 Craft Knife For general cutting and trimming. Always use on a cutting mat and have spare blades to hand.

19 Glass Cutter For cutting glass.

20 Bevel Edge Mount Cutter Hand-held tool for cutting bevelled edges in mount (mat) board.

21 Masking Tape Light sticking tape used for finishing off the back of a frame.

22 Frame Clamp Adjustable clamp to hold glued frames together during drying.

MOUNTS (MATS) & MOUNTING

The mount (mat) is a cardboard window which is placed on the artwork. It should not be confused with the backing board or card on which the artwork is stuck, although this is sometimes incorrectly referred to as the mount.

Mounts are more than purely decorative. They serve to prevent works on paper, whether they be water-colours, pastels or photographs, from being damaged by condensation, which can happen if they are left in direct contact with the frame.

Mounts were not widely used until the nineteenth century, when cardboard was produced industrially for the first time. Before this, works on paper had sometimes been protected from the glass by match-sized pieces of wood, which were inserted between the glass and the artwork. Another alternative to the mount was the slip frame: this was a bevelled, flat section of wood that was gilded or decorated to suit the picture. It would be slipped behind the glass and in front of the picture.

As a rule, the width of the mount at the bottom of the image should be greater than that at the top and sides. This is to compensate for an optical illusion that makes the space at the bottom of a picture appear smaller than the space at the top if they are actually equal. If this is not done, the picture will look as if it is sliding out of the mount or the frame.

The width of the mount has an effect on the picture as a whole. For example, in too small a mount a picture can look restricted and cramped. If the mount is large in comparison with the picture, the picture will look better sitting high up in the mount.

The colour of the mount will affect whether the picture looks as though it is about to jump out at you, or seems to recede into the wall and become lost. Some mounts will make a picture look darker; others will make it lighter. If you are unsure about what looks best, cut some mounts out of paper and paint them a variety of colours. Place them over the artwork to see which

looks best. When you have chosen, use that tone to make your mount.

Mountboard (mat board) is available in different thicknesses, known as "sheet" sizes. These range from four to ten, four-sheet being 1000 microns, six-sheet being 1250 microns and eight-sheet being 1900 microns thick. Six-sheet is the most commonly used thickness and is available in the widest range of colours. Most mounts are made with a bevelled edge. Instead of holding the craft knife vertically when you cut a piece of board, you angle it so that it cuts the edge at an angle or slope. Bevelling by hand can be quite difficult: a sharp cutting tool is essential and a metal rule can be used to cut against, but if possible it is preferable to use a hand-held mount cutter, a tool which holds replaceable blades in position.

Creating decorative mounts can be an art form in its own right. You can decorate mounts by painting them, or stick decorated papers on to them. Techniques as varied as marbling, gold leaf, sponging, spattering and stippling can be used for decorated papers; mounts may also be covered in fabric. Some of these techniques are covered in the *Painted Frames* chapter of this book, and the same methods can easily be used on mounts.

To marble a mount, simply float oil paint thinned with a little turps on top of a bath of water. Swirl the colour round to create a pattern, and then lay the mount on the colour. Lift it off vertically and the marbled pattern will stick to the mount.

Opposite: mounts (mats) may be plain or highly decorated. You can create your own designs by using different paint techniques such as sponging, dragging or stencilling.

MAKING MOUNTS

Before framing a picture, first cut the mount (mat). A mount usually has a bevelled or sloping edge, so that the eye is led into the picture. It is generally agreed that wide margins look better in neutral colours such as ivory, or pale cream and grey shades. A large area of a strong colour may swamp the image inside.

Before you start it is a good idea to make a diagram of the mount showing its proportions and measurements so that you can refer to it whilst you are working. The internal measurement where the artwork will be visible is known as the "sight area"; it must be at least 2.5 mm (⅛ in) smaller than the picture on each side. Mark the measurement on the diagram. Mark the measurements for the top and bottom and sides to calculate the overall size of mountboard (mat board) required. Remember that you must take into account the width of the rebate as it will cover the outer edges of the mount.

HINTS AND TIPS

■ When measuring the mount, place the board face-down and mark on the back of the board, so the front is left clean of any pencil lines.

■ Once you have drawn the window, and before you do any cutting, check it with a set square to make sure there are four right angles.

■ Make sure that the blades on the mount-cutter are razor-sharp, and keep spare blades to hand, to replace as soon as cutting becomes difficult.

■ Always cut mounts on a spare piece of card as bevelled cuts will not "heal" on a cutting mat.

MATERIALS
— AND —
EQUIPMENT

mountboard (mat board)
ruler
pencil
set square
metal rule (straight edge)
thick waste card
hand-held bevel edge mount-cutter
craft knife

1 Mark out the dimensions of the top, bottom, sides and sight area of the mount (mat) on the back of the mountboard (mat board). Place the board on a spare piece of thick waste card, not on a cutting mat. Position the steel rule (straight edge) and cutter and slide the blade out just enough to cut the mountboard. Move the blade up and down the line, increasing the depth of the cut with each stroke. Overcut the corners slightly.

2 If the window does not fall away use a craft knife to finish off the cut carefully.

MAKING FRAMES

A frame with mitred corners is the most traditional type. First work out the size of the frame you want, in order to calculate the amount of moulding to buy.

MEASURING & CALCULATING QUANTITIES

Measure the size of the work to be framed. The size will be the size of the frame between the rebates (rabbets) plus a cutting allowance of 2.5 mm (⅛ in). A useful formula for working out the amount of moulding is to add the all-round measurement of the artwork, plus eight times the width of the moulding, plus a small allowance for cutting.

HINTS AND TIPS

■ Whichever method you use to cut the moulding, it is important that the bottom surface is always in contact with the surface of the saw. If the bottom is tilted you will not get a 45-degree angle.

■ G-clamps help to hold an awkwardly shaped or a long piece of moulding in place.

■ If using a new mitre-saw, put a little grease on the surface of the blade to make it cut smoothly.

■ Hold the saw in a relaxed fashion and use light pressure: if you are heavy-handed, the saw will jump and you won't get a smooth cut.

MATERIALS AND EQUIPMENT

moulding
mitre-saw
ruler
pencil
hardboard
craft knife
frame-clamp
wood glue
panel pins
wire cutters
nails
hand drill
nail punch
tack hammer
wood filler
glass
cutting mat
chinagraph pencil (china marker)
metal T-square
glass-cutter
hardboard
hacksaw
masking tape
bradawl (awl)
screw-eyes
picture wire

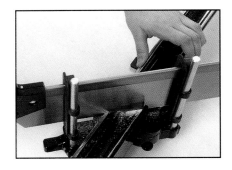

1 Cut a mitre at the end of the strip of moulding (see Figure 2). Measure the first long side along the rebate (rabbet) edge and mark the moulding. Replace the moulding on the mitre-saw, adjust the angle of the saw and make the second cut.

2 Adjust the angle of the saw again to cut off the waste piece of moulding (see Figure 2).

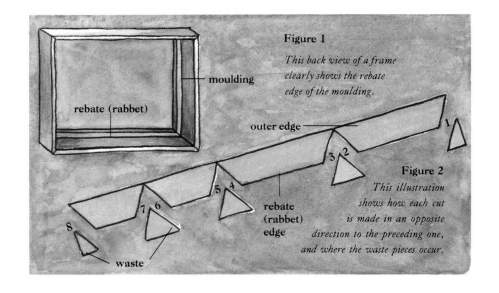

moulding

rebate (rabbet)

outer edge

rebate (rabbet) edge

waste

Figure 1

This back view of a frame clearly shows the rebate edge of the moulding.

Figure 2

This illustration shows how each cut is made in an opposite direction to the preceding one, and where the waste pieces occur.

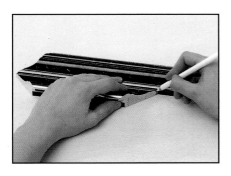
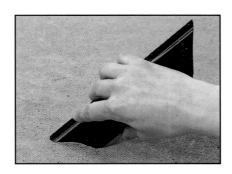

3 To mark off the second length, use the piece that has just been cut as a measure. Lay both pieces, back-to-back, on a flat surface and mark the outer edge of the moulding. Replace the moulding on the mitre-saw, line up the pencil mark with the cross cut on the base and cut out a second length. Repeat the whole procedure to cut the two shorter lengths of moulding.

4 Smooth the mitred edges by rubbing them on the rough side of the hardboard. Remove any whiskers with a sharp craft knife.

5 Arrange the frame-clamp loosely around the four strips of moulding, and glue the mitred edges together with wood glue.

6 Carefully tighten the clamp and wipe off any excess glue that appears from the joints inside and out. If the outside edge of the moulding is very narrow, you may find it easier to place the frame on a piece of hardboard to raise it slightly and allow the corners of the clamp a firmer grip. Leave to dry.

7 To pin the frame, cut off the head of a pin with the wire cutters and use the shaft as a drill bit. Drill the pin into the side of the frame. The pins need to be long enough to cross the join and hold the two pieces of wood together. If the frame is to hold a heavy object, such as a mirror, you will need to put two pins in each joint.

8 Use a nail punch and a hammer to insert the final length of pin. Fill the hole with coloured filler. If the frame is to be stained, use a wood filler that will take the stain.

CUTTING
THE GLASS

1 Always cut glass on a cutting mat. Mark the dimensions of the required piece on the edge of the glass with a chinagraph pencil (china marker). Position the T-square and score down it with a glass-cutter.

2 To break the glass, place a pencil slightly to one side of the scored line underneath the sheet of glass. Press down firmly on either side with both hands.

There are many different fixings available for hanging frames. Screw-eyes and picture wire are simplest to use, but for heavy frames or mirrors use hanging plates.

FINISHING OFF
THE FRAME

1 Cut the hardboard to fit the back of the frame, using a hacksaw or craft knife. Position the hardboard in the frame and secure it with panel pins all the way round.

2 Stick masking tape round the edge of the frame so that it also covers the pins. This neatens the appearance of the back of the frame and protects the picture from dust and dirt as well.

3 Decide which way you wish to hang the frame and fix the screw-eyes into the moulding a quarter of the way from the top. It is easier to screw them in if you first make a hole with a bradawl (awl) or hammer and nail. When the rings are secure, attach a double-length of picture wire.

BASIC FRAME ELEMENTS

frame

glass

mount
(mat)

picture

backing
board

*Left: this illustration shows how all
the individual elements of a basic frame
are put together.*

*Below: these wooden frames of differing
sizes and shapes look very effective hung
in an informal group. When hanging
frames, do bear in mind where the main
light source is in the room. If your
picture is opposite a window it may be
best to use non-reflective glass.*

REPAIR & RENOVATION

There are many things that can go wrong with a frame: the glass may crack, the joints can loosen and the wood itself may start to rot or have woodworm. Pieces may fall off and need to be remade. However, most frames can be mended with a little care and attention.

Before you rush in and mend everything in sight, though, do be cautious. If the frame you own is old, it might be valuable; if so, it's best to have it mended by an expert.

GLASS

A picture which looks dull and dingy may only be suffering from dirty glass or nicotine stains on the glass. Remove these by washing the glass with a proprietary (commercial) glass cleaner. If this doesn't work, try using wire wool soaked in methylated spirits (denatured alcohol). If this last treatment doesn't clean the glass you will have to replace it. To dismantle the frame, place it face-down on a clean, soft surface. Remove the tacks from the back that hold the backing and picture in place. Lift up the picture and then remove the glass. Use the old piece as a size-guide for the new piece.

OLD PAINT

If the frame has a painted or varnished finish which is in poor condition, the finish can usually be removed with paint stripper. After you remove the paint stripper, fill any nicks or holes in the wood with wood filler and then sand down the frame.

MOULDINGS

If a piece of an ornate plaster frame has broken off, it can usually be re-glued with wood glue. If a piece is missing, either carve or mould a new one by hand, using a self-hardening clay, or make another piece as follows:

Press an area of the frame similar to the one missing into a piece of Plasticine. Press the modelling material into the Plasticine mould and allow it to set. When it's hard, remove it and cut and sand it to fit into the gap. Glue with wood glue and then paint with gold or an ordinary paint to match the rest of the frame.

LOOSE JOINTS

If the frame has loose joints, gently prise the frame apart by holding one length of moulding in a vice (vise), protected by pieces of wood, and gently tap the adjacent piece away from it with a hammer and a block of wood. Remove any pins using pliers. Remove old glue from the ends of the moulding by gently sanding, being careful not to round off the ends. Reassemble the frame using glue and a frame-clamp.

LACQUER FRAMES

These can sometimes be chipped or scratched. If the gesso underneath is chipped or broken, apply new coats of gesso. This can be bought in a quick-drying acrylic form. When the gesso is dry, apply a coat of varnish.

REPAIRING PLASTER

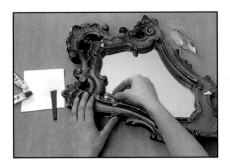

1 Mend an old plaster frame by first glueing on any pieces which have dropped off.

2 Push self-hardening clay into any other small parts which have dropped off and mould it to follow the lines of the frame. Leave to dry.

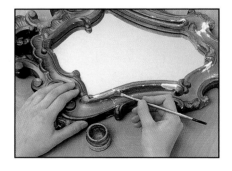

3 Give the white clay mends a fresh coat of colour using gold powder mixed with turpentine solution. Alternatively, you could also use matching gold paint or lacquer.

STRIPPING

1 A heavily painted frame can be stripped for repainting. First, apply paint stripper with a brush. Protect your hands with gloves.

2 Leave the paint stripper on for as long as advised in the manufacturer's instructions. Remove the paint with a scraper and wire wool. An old toothbrush is useful for working on detailed areas.

RETOUCHING

1 An old, non-valuable papier-mâché frame can be touched up using a very fine brush and acrylic paints. Do not attempt to repair antiques yourself in this manner – they will require professional mending.

2 Apply a new coat of varnish to the surface of the frame, giving it a gloss finish.

RENOVATING

1 For an old wooden frame in need of repair, first remove old rusty tacks with a pair of pliers and then strip any old paper off the back.

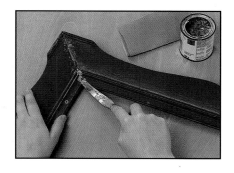

2 Check the front of the frame for loose joins and use wood filler where needed. When the wood filler is dry, sand down the whole of the frame. Apply two or three coats of paint and varnish the whole frame.

ADAPTING FRAMES

You may have been given a work of art that you want to hang and can't afford a new frame. Old frames can be adapted and decorated to make them into something wonderful. Even the humble clip frame can be given different decorative surrounds. Here are some ideas.

To decorate clip frames save wine corks, cut them in half and then stick them round the outside edge of the

Right: adapt a square frame by cutting off the corners to make a more interesting shape.

glass. Make a doilly-edged frame by cutting strips from the outside of a rectangular paper doilly and sticking them under the edge of a clip frame. Metal foil can be embossed, by drawing on the back of the foil with a ballpoint pen and then cutting out the shape with scissors. The result can be used to adapt yet another clip frame.

An old wooden frame can be transformed by painting; add mosaic, twigs, fabric or anything else you like to decorate the frame. The frame could be cut down to make a smaller frame. Or you can add a *bas-relief* pattern made from self-hardening clay, or by forming papier-mâché shapes from kitchen paper (paper towels) rolled in glue. A broad frame could have its edges cut off at an angle to make a more interesting shape. A plain wooden frame could have cardboard shapes stuck on to it and then be covered with layers of papier-mâché and decorated in a number of different ways, including découpage, gold leaf or crackle-glazing. A tired-looking velvet frame could be embellished with beads or sequins or by gluing a coil of fine silken cord round it.

FRAME WITH PAPIER-MÂCHÉ SURROUND

1 From cardboard cut out the edge shape you desire for the frame. Using wood glue or masking tape, stick the cardboard on to the frame.

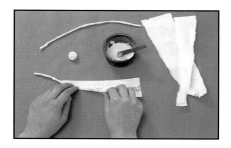

2 Cover the frame and cardboard extensions with strips of glued newspaper. Coat the tissue paper with glue and roll it into spirals and balls.

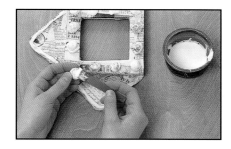

3 Glue the spirals to the rim of the cardboard extensions and the balls around the face of the wooden frame. Leave to dry.

4 Paint with a coat of acrylic gesso. Leave to dry then paint with blue acrylic paint. Finish by painting on a gold pattern and rubbing gold powder on to the paper balls.

Opposite: give a flat frame some interest and contrasting colour by adding an inner frame of narrow beading. Measure and cut four mitred lengths of beading. Arrange the lengths within a frame clamp and glue together. Tighten the clamp and leave to dry overnight. Stick the beading frame on to the front of the flat-faced frame.

Right: give a plain wooden frame a new lease of life using a cardboard cut-out, edged and decorated with tissue paper and papier-mâché. Paint it in dark blue with gold highlights.

Hanging Frames

The design of frames and pictures has evolved over the years, and so too have the ways in which they are displayed. Historic ways of hanging can seem very odd to us today. For example, in the seventeenth century paintings were often hung much higher than they are today; sometimes they were just below the ceiling. The pictures would be angled forward in order that people standing below could see the painting properly. Paintings would be hung directly over tapestries – which were there for warmth and insulation as well as ornament – and often indiscriminately nailed through.

During the eighteenth century, paintings were hung in architecturally precise groups. Pictures were hung on chains and were arranged so as to look good on the wall rather than for the convenience of the spectator. The furniture designer Thomas Sheraton was the first to suggest that the height of pictures should take into account viewing considerations.

By the nineteenth century pictures were hung less formally in tiers by cord or wire. As the century progressed, and all the decorative arts became more elaborate, so did styles of hanging pictures. Sometimes they were hung by cords from studs covered with silk bows or rosettes. Sometimes the cord would be covered with the same fabric as the rosette. By the end of the century, there was a backlash against the over-ornate high-Victorian style. The 'Aesthetic' or Arts and Crafts movement was born, and with it a new vogue for displaying paintings on artist's easels.

As with all matters of style, things are more relaxed nowadays. There are a few practical guidelines worth bearing in mind when hanging pictures, however. Oil paintings should never be hung directly above radiators, because heat can damage the surface of the painting. The heat of the radiator can cause dust and grime to rise, causing yet more damage. Only paintings covered in glass should be hung over a heat source.

Works of art can be damaged by damp and condensation, so bathrooms are inhospitable places for them. Sunlight will fade water-colours and some gouache paints, so do not hang paintings in these media in direct sunlight. In tight spaces, hang small-scale works of art which need to be viewed close to. Choose large rooms for large paintings, so you can stand back to view them properly.

If you have a collection of odd pieces of art that you want to hang together, choose identical frames, or at least frames of a similar colour or made by the same technique, to give a feeling of unity. One way of aligning pictures of different sizes and proportions is to line up either the tops or the bottoms of the picture frames.

Left: an Oxford frame is secured by two silk tassles and hung from a hook.

Opposite: the frame is hung by ruched fabric in soft green, chosen to complement the print.

*The equestrian theme of this picture is
extended to the way in which
it has been hung.*

*Above: plastic coat hangers in bright
primary colours are an inexpensive and
fun way to hang children's pictures.
Here we have used colour co-ordinating
duffle coat fasteners to suspend the
picture from the coat hanger.*

*Opposite: light fixtures or candle sconces
may be used for hanging pictures from.
In this case the colour of the beeswax
candles is enhanced by the colour of
the frame. Always check that the wall
fixture can support the weight
of the frame.*

For awkward places such as staircases,
where this is not possible, line up the
pictures in vertical columns or just
mass them together tightly so the wall
is completely covered.

Group similar types of work
together, for example, prints or water-
colours; this will have a much stronger
visual impact than a single picture on
its own. Or hang pictures together
that are connected by theme, for
example animal or botanical prints.

A useful tip for grouping pictures
to the best effect is to arrange and
rearrange them on the floor until you
have a balance you like, and then hang
the pictures on the wall.

Frames do not have to be hung
squarely; an interesting idea is to turn
the frame on its side to make a
diamond shape, and then cut the
mount so the picture will show
through in the right alignment.

Natural plaits of woven hessian or
raffia make a good hanging for
pictures, as does tartan ribbon topped
with a bow or a rosette. Dressing-
gown cord and tassels can be used for
hanging ornate frames. A *trompe l'oeil*

effect may be achieved by
découpaging a bow on to a wall and
hanging the picture below to look as
though it is hung from the bow. I have
even seen pictures hung to look as if
from bows of builder's scrim, a very
coarsely woven ribbon used in
plastering. Imagination is all!

The most common method of
hanging uses ready-made braided wire
and screw-eyes. These are available in
different grades, according to the size
and weight of the frame. Sometimes
D-rings are used instead of screw-
eyes; these allow the picture to hang
flat against the wall. Smaller pictures
can be hung from a sawtooth hanger.
Pictures can be hung from picture
rails or just from the wall. All but the
smallest frames will hang better from
a picture hook than from a nail driven
straight into the wall.

PAINTED FRAMES

 THE FRAMES IN THIS CHAPTER OF THE BOOK ARE THE MOST TRADITIONAL THAT YOU WILL FIND IN THE BOOK – BUT THERE ARE STILL SOME UNUSUAL IDEAS. THE TECHNIQUES AND STYLES OF FINISH ARE VARIED, AND COVER THE TRADITIONAL DECORATOR'S TECHNIQUES OF STAINING, DRAGGING, SPONGING AND STIPPLING. THESE CAN BE DONE QUICKLY AND WITHOUT ANY SPECIALIZED EQUIPMENT. THE SLIGHTLY MORE COMPLEX TECHNIQUES OF MARBLING, STENCILLING AND VERDIGRIS ARE ALSO SHOWN, ALL WITH CLEAR STEP-BY-STEP PHOTOGRAPHS. THE MOST COMPLICATED OF ALL THE TECHNIQUES IS THE GILDED FRAME, BUT IF YOU USE ACRYLIC GESSO EVEN THIS IS EASY. TAKE NOTICE OF DRYING TIMES, AND DO NOT APPLY TOO MUCH PAINT AT ONCE.

Left: three frames by a textile designer. On the left, a simple plaid design in a wash of grey on white. On the right, spirals are drawn on to the frame with a felt-tip pen, then painted with a wash of water to create a smudged, softened look. In the centre, the design is sketched boldly in pencil and then over-painted with gold acrylic. (Hermione Carline)

Right: the natural world, both land and sea, is the inspiration for this artistry. The frames are made from pine. (Rebecca Campbell)

Above: this frame is painted with several layers of emulsion (latex), stained and then treated with a crackle glaze. (James Ellis Stevens)

Right: in the foreground, a pine frame which has been gilded and then rubbed down to create a distressed effect. (Gentle and Boon) The wooden frame behind has been oil gilded with copper leaf and given a verdigris finish. Because of lack of space, one word has been omitted from the famous quotation by Francis Bacon that runs round the frame; "There is no [excellent] beauty that hath not some strangeness in the proportion". (Lily Curtis)

Below: the colours of the frame reflect those in the picture but are muted so that they don't detract from it. (James Ellis Stevens)

Above: this rustic frame made from sawn pine has been stained and sponged. A narrow wooden slip frame has been used in place of a mount (mat). (James Ellis Stevens)

STAINING, STIPPLING, DRAGGING & SPONGING

Four frames decorated using different paint techniques. Top left: sponging. Top right: stippling a dark colour on top of a light one. Bottom left: drag a brush through a nearly dry colour on top of a different colour. Bottom right: staining. (Josephine Whitfield)

THE FOUR PAINT TECHNIQUES SHOWN HERE ARE SIMPLE TO ACHIEVE AND VERY EFFECTIVE. ALWAYS ALLOW THE BASE COAT TO DRY THOROUGHLY.

MATERIALS
— AND —
EQUIPMENT

four wooden frames
paintbrush
emulsion (latex) paints
cloth
acrylic paint
stippling brush
masking tape
sponge

STAINING

Paint on a white emulsion (latex) paint base coat. Leave to dry. Paint on top with a diluted dark blue emulsion and then rub it off with a cloth, while it is still wet.

STIPPLING

Paint on a base coat of light green emulsion. Dip a stippling brush in to some dark green acrylic paint. Dab off excess paint and then lightly stipple on top of the light green base coat.

DRAGGING

Paint on a pale peach emulsion base coat. Mask off the corners to achieve crisp 45-degree angles. Paint on a second coat in a deeper shade. Drag the brush through the paint before it dries. Paint one side at a time.

SPONGING

Paint on a cream emulsion base coat. Mix up some light-brown paint. Dip a sponge in the brown paint and then dab excess off on to a spare piece of paper. Sponge the paint on to the frame.

DISTRESSED PAINT MIRROR FRAME

To achieve this rustic, two-tone effect, the frame is painted with two colours of emulsion (latex) paint, with a layer of furniture polish in the middle. The whole frame is sanded and where the wax polish lies, the top layer of paint comes away. (Josephine Whitfield)

WAX POLISH CAN BE USED TO CREATE A BARRIER BETWEEN TWO COATS OF PAINT WHICH ARE THEN RUBBED WITH SANDPAPER TO CREATE AN INTERESTING EFFECT. MINGLE THE TWO COLOURS IN A BALANCE THAT SEEMS PLEASING TO YOU.

MATERIALS
— AND —
EQUIPMENT

frame with mirror

masking tape

white, light green and blue emulsion (latex) paint

paintbrush

wax polish

soft cloth

sandpaper

1 Protect the mirror with masking tape. Paint the frame with white emulsion (latex) and then give it a coat of light green. Leave to dry.

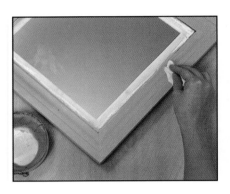

2 Rub wax polish all over the surface of the frame with a cloth. Leave to dry.

3 Paint a coat of blue emulsion over the wax and leave to dry.

4 When the paint is dry, rub over the whole surface with sandpaper to reveal the colour beneath. Remove the masking tape.

VERDIGRIS FRAME

THIS LOOK OF AGED COPPER IS ACHIEVED BY USING GREEN AND METALLIC ACRYLIC PAINTS TO SIMULATE THE GREEN DEPOSIT WHICH FORMS ON COPPER OR BRASS THAT HAS BEEN EXPOSED TO THE ELEMENTS AND OXIDIZED.

By clever use of paint, an old mirror frame is given a new lease of life and a fashionable verdigris look. Iridescent copper paint is the base coat, with a mixture of emerald, black and white paint as a top coat. (Josephine Whitfield)

MATERIALS
— AND —
EQUIPMENT

frame

iridescent copper, emerald green, white and black acrylic paint

paintbrush

soft cloth

1 Paint the frame with iridescent copper acrylic.

2 Mix emerald green with white and paint on to the iridescent frame randomly.

3 Whilst the paint is wet, remove some of the green colour with a cloth, for a textured look.

4 Paint on some small areas of black acrylic and rub the paint in with your fingers.

CRACKLE-VARNISHED ANTIQUED FRAME

Crackle varnishing is a method of ageing a frame using a special varnish. Two varnishes with different drying times are painted on top of one another, which causes cracking or crazing. To enhance this effect, a dark coloured oil paint is rubbed into the cracks.
(Josephine Whitfield)

BY USING ANTIQUE VARNISH WITH A CRACKLE VARNISH AND RUBBING RAW UMBER OIL PAINT IN TO THE CRACKS, YOU CAN GIVE A FRAME AN AIR OF AGED DISTINCTION.

MATERIALS
— AND —
EQUIPMENT

frame
wood filler and wood glue, if necessary
white emulsion (latex) paint
paintbrush
antique varnish
crackle varnish
raw umber oil paint
soft cloth

1 If the frame is old, repair it with wood filler and glue. Paint the frame with one or two coats of white emulsion (latex) paint.

2 Apply one coat of antique varnish to the frame.

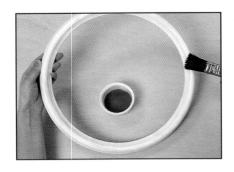

3 When the antique varnish is dry to the touch, apply a coat of crackle varnish. The cracks may take a long time to appear: it depends on the humidity of the room. To speed up the process, place the frame over a heat source for a few moments.

4 When the cracks appear, rub raw umber oil paint into the cracks, using the cloth. Let the paint dry for 10 minutes.

5 Apply a second coat of antique varnish to seal and protect the finish.

FLORAL STENCIL MIRROR FRAME

 THIS FRAME IS INSPIRED BY THE TRADITIONAL FOLK-ART MOTIFS OF FLOWERS AND LEAVES, AND IS PARTICULARLY SUITED TO A RUSTIC-STYLE FRAME.

MATERIALS
— AND —
EQUIPMENT

frame with mirror
masking tape
white emulsion (latex) paint
paintbrush
clear acetate film
black magic marker pen
cutting mat
craft knife
green and red acrylic paint
stencilling brush
acrylic varnish

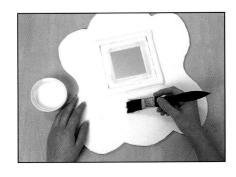

1 Protect the mirror edges with masking tape. Paint the frame with white emulsion (latex).

2 Using the templates on page 152, draw the stencil design on to clear acetate film, using the black pen.

3 Cut out the stencil on the cutting mat, using the craft knife.

4 Use masking tape to hold the stem and leaf stencil in position. To stencil, dip the stencilling brush in the green paint and stamp off any excess on a spare piece of paper. If the brush is too wet the design can easily smudge. When you have completed one side of the frame, flip the stencil over to complete the other side. Leave to dry.

5 Stencil the red parts of the design, the flowers. Leave to dry.

6 Mask off the leaves on the leaf stencil with tape and use the stem shape to stencil the curvy lines round the mirror edge. Leave to dry. Paint the whole frame with a coat of clear varnish, and when dry remove the masking tape from the mirror.

A pretty stencilled frame suitable for a country kitchen or perhaps a young girl's room. The broad edge allows plenty of room for decoration. (Josephine Whitfield)

MARBLE-EFFECT MIRROR FRAME

*The uneven markings and crazing
naturally occurring in marble can be
copied with the skilful application of
paint, using a paintbrush and a feather.
(Josephine Whitfield)*

THIS WOODEN FRAME IS CHANGED BEYOND RECOGNITION BY USING THE DECORATING TECHNIQUE OF MARBLING, TO GIVE A STONE-LIKE EFFECT TO THE SURROUND.

MATERIALS
— AND —
EQUIPMENT

masking tape

frame with mirror

white eggshell paint

paintbrush

white, raw umber and sap green oil paint

turpentine

linseed oil

rag

goose feather

soft brush

1 Stick masking tape along the inner edge of the frame to protect the mirror. Coat the frame with a layer of white eggshell paint, and leave until completely dry.

2 Mix the raw umber and sap green paints with the turpentine and linseed oil. Paint on to the frame and take off excess paint with the rag to create a textured look.

3 Put the end of the goose feather into a mixture of turpentine and sap green and white oil paint. Draw lines on to the frame with the feather.

4 Make up another mixture of raw umber and sap green with a smaller amount of turpentine and linseed oil for a stronger hue. Draw more lines on to the frame, varying the pressure on the feather.

5 Brush over the damp frame with a soft brush to bring the textures together for a marbled effect.

PAINTED GRAPE MOTIF MIRROR FRAME

Luscious grapes and vine leaves are hand-painted on this frame. The design is first drawn on to a template and then transferred to the frame at the corners before the painting begins.
(Josephine Whitfield)

WITH THE USE OF A TEMPLATE AND TRACING PAPER, YOU CAN HAND-PAINT A FRAME TO LOOK AS GOOD AS IF IT WERE DONE BY AN ARTIST.

MATERIALS
— AND —
EQUIPMENT

frame with mirror

masking tape

paintbrushes

white emulsion (latex) paint

pencil

tracing paper

coloured chalk

purple, sap green, white and raw umber acrylic paint

oak-coloured antique varnish

cloth

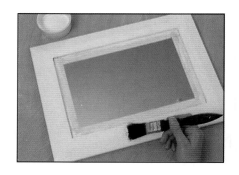

1 Put masking tape round the edge of the mirror to protect it. Paint the frame with three coats of white emulsion (latex).

2 Using a pencil, trace the grape design from page 152 on to tracing paper. Rub chalk on to the back of the tracing. Place the design on the corners of the frame and go over the lines with the pencil, to transfer the design on to the frame.

3 Dilute the purple and green acrylic paints with water. Using a fine brush, paint in a wash of purple for the grapes and a wash of sap green for the leaves.

4 Add white to the purple acrylic to paint the highlights on the grapes. Add white to the sap green paint and add highlights to the leaves.

5 Paint round the edges of the fruit and leaves with raw umber paint using a very fine brush. When the paint is dry, apply a coat of antique varnish and rub off any excess with a cloth, for an "antique" effect.

SUNNY DAISY·FRAME

THIS VIBRANT PAINTED FRAME WITH FLOWERS OF
CHILDLIKE SIMPLICITY IS FURTHER ENHANCED
BY GILDED SWIRLS. THE *SGRAFFITO* EFFECT IS ACHIEVED
BY PARTIALLY SANDING AWAY THE TOP COAT OF PAINT.

*This wooden frame with attractive
curved moulding is hand-painted with
a simple daisy design. Once varnished,
it was decorated with gilded swirls
down both sides in the form of transfer
gold leaf. This is easily applied by
rubbing it on to a base of 3-hour size
with your finger. (Louise Gardam)*

MATERIALS
—— AND ——
EQUIPMENT

acrylic gesso

frame

paintbrushes

ultramarine, cobalt blue, titanium white
and cadmium yellow acrylic paint

coarse sandpaper

cloth

satin varnish

3-hour size

book of transfer gold leaf
(or Dutch metal)

1 Paint the acrylic gesso on to the
frame in thin layers with a damp
paintbrush. The gesso takes about 30
minutes to dry between coats; you need
to apply four coats in order to form a
solid base coat for the frame.

2 When the last coat of gesso is dry,
mix some of the ultramarine and
cobalt blue acrylic paint and paint over
the gesso base coat.

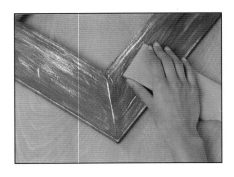

3 Rub back the frame with coarse
sandpaper to create a scratched
sgraffito effect. Buff with a dry cloth.
Be careful not to get the gesso wet or it
will dissolve.

4 Paint four loose, freehand daisy
flowers in the corners, with white
and yellow acrylic paints, using a fine
brush. Paint a design of stitches round
the edge of the frame in white. When
the design is dry, give the frame a coat
of satin varnish.

5 When the varnish is dry, gild the
frame by painting 3-hour size
swirls on to it. When the size is tacky,
place the transfer gold leaf on top and
rub gently with your finger. The gold
leaf will adhere to the size in the shape
of the swirl. Dry for 24 hours.

PAPER FRAMES

 PAPER IS NOT THE MEDIUM WHICH FIRST SPRINGS TO MIND FOR FRAME-MAKING. HOWEVER, IT IS A VERY VERSATILE MEDIUM AND COMES IN MANY THICKNESSES AND TEXTURES. SOME OF THE FRAMES IN THIS SECTION ARE CONSTRUCTED JUST FROM PAPER, OTHERS FROM CARDBOARD AND OTHERS FROM PAPIER-MÂCHÉ. WHEN LOOKING AT THE PROJECTS, YOU WILL BE SURPRISED AT JUST HOW MANY DIFFERENT FRAMES CAN BE MADE FROM PAPER.

MANY OF THE MATERIALS USED TO PRODUCE THESE FRAMES ARE THINGS THAT YOU WILL HAVE AT HOME ALREADY, SUCH AS WRAPPING PAPER, CARDBOARD BOXES AND NEWSPAPER. SO, IF YOU ARE FEELING IMPOVERISHED *AND* IN NEED OF INSPIRATION THIS IS THE CHAPTER TO LOOK FOR ECONOMICAL PRESENT IDEAS.

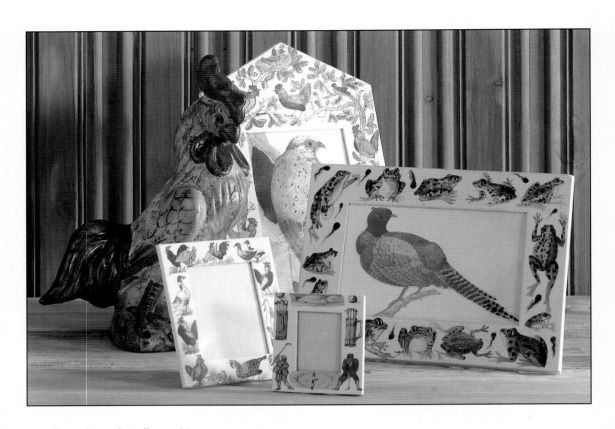

*Above: these ecologically-sound frames
are made from re-cycled paper and
cardboard, and decorated with charming
wildlife and sporting prints.
(Matthew Rice)*

*Above: a papier-mâché frame made to
celebrate an engagement. The "gems"
and the ring are raised up on the face of
the frame. (Kirsti Rees)*

Below: a corrugated cardboard frame
embellished with string, scrunched paper
and a capital A. (Kirsti Rees)

Above: the shapes on the surfaces of
these papier-mâché mirror frames are
cut from cardboard and then layered
with papier-mâché before being stuck on
to the frames. The backgrounds are
painted different colours, layered one
upon another, before being distressed
by sanding. (Hannah Downes)

Left: pulped papier-mâché, a very
strong and bold medium, is the basis for
these frames which are influenced by
the sea and sand of the Caribbean.
The golden shells shine as if glinting in
the sun. (Sue Sanders)

TWISTED-PAPER FRAME

A circular cardboard frame is covered with unravelled twisted paper. The paper is simply stuck into position. The surface of the frame is spattered with paint and when dry decorated with stars. (Dorothy Wood)

THIS FRAME IS MADE FROM UNRAVELLED TWISTED PAPER, WHICH IS AVAILABLE FROM QUALITY GIFT-WRAP SHOPS.

MATERIALS
—— AND ——
EQUIPMENT

plate and saucer to draw round
pencil
cardboard
scissors
cutting mat
craft knife
twisted paper
PVA (white) glue
gold and white emulsion (latex) paint
old toothbrush
fabric star motifs
cardboard for backing (optional)

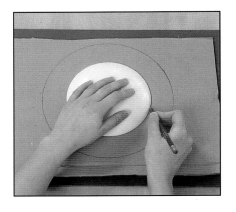

1 Draw round the plate on to the piece of cardboard. Place the saucer in the centre of the circle you have just drawn and draw round this.

2 Cut out the outer circle with a pair of scissors and then the inner circle using a craft knife, so you are left with a cardboard ring.

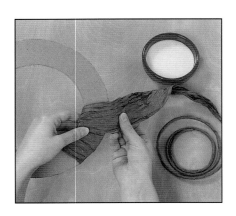

3 Unwind the twisted paper and wind it round the ring until the ring is fully covered. Stick the end down with PVA (white) glue.

4 Put the white and gold paint in to two saucers. Place the frame on paper to protect the work surface. Dip the toothbrush into the white paint and then run your finger along the bristles so a fine spray of paint lands on the frame. Repeat with the gold paint.

5 Stick the star motifs all over the frame, again using PVA glue. If you wish, stick a cardboard backing circle on the back, leaving a gap through which to insert the picture.

CORRUGATED CARDBOARD FRAME

 CARDBOARD IS A WONDERFUL MEDIUM FOR MAKING INTERESTING FRAMES. IT IS A CHEAP AND VERSATILE MATERIAL THAT CAN BE BRIGHTLY PAINTED, OR LEFT PLAIN IF YOU PREFER NATURAL TEXTURES AND COLOURS.

MATERIALS
— AND —
EQUIPMENT

pencil
ruler
scissors
cardboard box
cutting mat
craft knife
corrugated cardboard
gold and red acrylic paint
paintbrush
PVA (white) glue

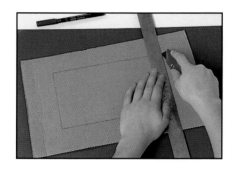

1 Cut out two pieces of box cardboard the same size, one for the backing and one for the frame. Draw a frame on one piece and cut out the window with a craft knife.

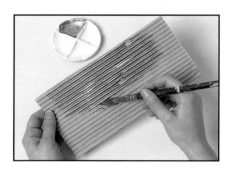

2 Paint some of the corrugated cardboard gold.

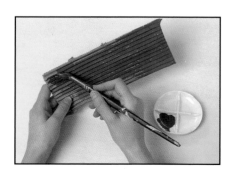

3 Paint some of the corrugated cardboard red.

4 Draw holly berries on the red cardboard and cut them out.

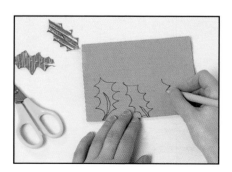

5 Draw holly leaves freehand on the gold and unpainted brown cardboard and cut them out with a slit down the centre, to indicate the central vein of the leaf.

6 Arrange the leaves and berries on to the cardboard frame and glue them in place.

7 Stick the frame on to the backing on three sides, leaving the fourth side open. Feed your photograph or picture in through this slot.

Even the most humble of materials may be used to create fun frames. Here different thicknesses of corrugated card have been cut in to leaf and berry shapes, and the variation above uses crumpled paper sprayed with gold paint to add further texture to a simple cardboard frame. (Juliet Bawden)

MIRROR FRAME WITH FLOWER DÉCOUPAGE

Découpage, the art of cutting, gluing and varnishing, is used here to good effect to hide the signs of ageing on both the mirror and its frame.
(Josephine Whitfield)

 DÉCOUPAGE IS THE ART OF DECORATING A SURFACE WITH CUT-OUT PAPER IMAGES. THE IMAGES ARE PROTECTED BY MANY LAYERS OF VARNISH. IT IS A USEFUL AND ATTRACTIVE METHOD FOR COVERING MARKS ON OLD FRAMES.

MATERIALS
— AND —
EQUIPMENT

frame with mirror
masking tape
green emulsion (latex) paint
paintbrushes
scissors
floral wrapping paper
raw umber acrylic paint
wood glue
antique varnish

1 Protect the mirror with masking tape. Paint the frame with two coats of green emulsion (latex).

2 Cut out flower motifs from the wrapping paper.

3 Paint the back of the flowers that you want to stick on the mirror with a dark colour, in this case raw umber. This stops the white back of the flowers reflecting in the mirror.

4 Remove the masking tape. Stick the motifs around the mirror frame and on to the mirror.

5 Give the frame a coat of antique varnish; this will give the whole thing a warm mellow colour. Allow to dry and repeat three times more.

PAPIER-MÂCHÉ FRAME

⬛ THIS FRAME IS CONSTRUCTED AROUND A
CARDBOARD BASE THAT IS SCORED WITH A KNIFE
BEFORE BEING FOLDED. LAYERS OF PAPIER-MÂCHÉ ARE
ADDED AND THE FRAME IS DECORATED USING CLAY THAT
HARDENS BY ITSELF, WITHOUT FIRING.

MATERIALS
— AND —
EQUIPMENT

pencil
tracing paper
ruler
cardboard
craft knife
masking tape
wire
wallpaper paste
newspaper
white emulsion (latex) paint
paintbrushes
self-hardening clay
clay-modelling tool
royal blue, violet and yellow poster paints
clear varnish
PVA (white) glue

1 Trace the template on page 157 and cut out the frame from the cardboard. Cut out the centre square and save it. This will be used to fix your picture on and make the backing for the frame. Score along the dotted lines using a craft knife. Be careful not to cut right through.

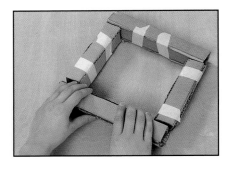

2 Fold each flap inwards along the scored edges and tape the frame together with masking tape.

3 Fix a piece of wire to the back, using masking tape. Mix up the wallpaper paste according to the manufacturer's instructions.

4 Tear the newspaper into pieces about 2.5 cm (1 in) square. Dip the squares in the paste and stick them on the frame until both the front and the back of the frame are covered.

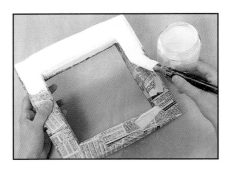

5 Prime the frame with white emulsion (latex) and leave it to dry. Give the frame a second coat of emulsion, to make sure that the surface is opaque. Leave this to dry.

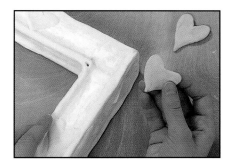

6 Decorate the front with self-hardening clay. Form heart shapes by hand and push these on to the frame. Fix them in place by smoothing down the sides of the hearts with a clay-modelling tool.

7 Paint with poster paints and leave to dry. Paint with a coat of varnish. Stick your painting or photo on the backing card set aside in step 1 and glue or tape it in place.

A simple cardboard-constructed frame, covered with layers of papier-mâché and decorated with self-hardening clay to form a three-dimensional heart motif border. The colours used here are strong and individual: use softer colours if you prefer. (Amanda Blunden)

EMBOSSED PAPER HEART MIRROR FRAME

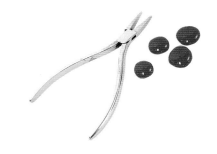

THIS OPULENT FRAME IS MADE FROM WATER-COLOUR PAPER WHICH HAS BEEN COATED WITH POSTER PAINT AND PVA (WHITE) GLUE. THE DECORATIVE PATTERN IS ACHIEVED BY SCORING THROUGH THE GLUE WITH THE END OF A PAINTBRUSH.

MATERIALS
— AND —
EQUIPMENT

tracing paper

pencil

300 lb rough water-colour paper

scissors

craft knife

cutting mat

crimson poster paint

paintbrush

PVA (white) glue

4 red glass nuggets

jeweller's pliers

gold wax

thick sharp needle and thread

silk tassel with bead

mirror tile

masking tape

strong paper for backing

strong glue

1 Trace the template from page 157 and use this as a guide to cut out the heart-shaped frame from the water-colour paper. Use scissors for the outside and a craft knife and cutting mat on the inside. Paint the frame with crimson poster paint.

2 Cover the frame in a thin layer of PVA (white) glue. Working quickly, use the paintbrush handle to mark patterns through the PVA, so the red paint shows through.

3 Stick the red glass shapes on to the PVA at the top and bottom of the heart shape.

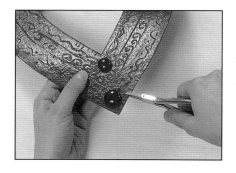

4 When the PVA is dry and transparent, crimp the edges using jeweller's pliers.

5 Gently rub on gold wax with your fingertip to cover the whole frame. Be sparing with the wax as you just want to highlight the pattern, not fill in the grooves.

6 With a thick, sharp needle, make a hole in the bottom of the frame and fasten on the tassel and bead with strong thread. Place the mirror tile behind the frame and stick it on to the frame, using masking tape around the edge. Use the heart-shaped template to cut out the backing paper. Cover one side of the backing paper with strong glue and fix it to the back of the frame.

This heart-shaped frame is brightly painted and then covered with a layer of PVA (white) glue into which patterns are scored with a sharp implement. Gold wax is rubbed on when the glue dries, to enhance the pattern. (Gill Clement)

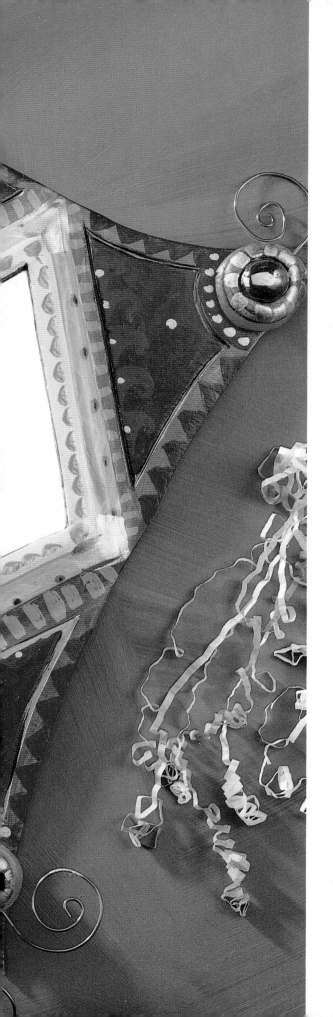

SCULPTED FRAMES

 SCULPTURE IS A THREE-DIMENSIONAL ART FORM. THESE SCULPTED FRAMES MAKE USE OF A VARIETY OF MALLEABLE MEDIA – SUCH AS POLYMER CLAY, SELF-HARDENING CLAY AND SALT DOUGH – THAT CAN BE SHAPED BY HAND, WITHOUT ANY COMPLICATED MOULDING, SCULPTING OR CASTING TECHNIQUES.

SELF-HARDENING CLAY IS EASY TO USE AND DOES NOT NEED AN OVEN OR A KILN TO FIRE IT. POLYMER CLAY COMES ALREADY COLOURED AND IS BAKED IN A DOMESTIC OVEN TO HARDEN IT. IT IS QUITE EXPENSIVE, BUT A LITTLE GOES A VERY LONG WAY. SALT DOUGH IS CHEAP AND EASY TO MAKE AND WORK WITH. ALL THESE MATERIALS CAN BE USED TO MAKE ENTIRE FRAMES, OR FOR SCULPTING DECORATIVE MOTIFS TO EMBELLISH EXISTING ONES.

Below: a circular ceramic frame with antique gold decoration and a handmade gold-lustred mirror. A small satellite mirror hangs below the main frame from a silk cord. (Tim and Karen Buzzard)

Above: this mirror frame is cast from plaster of Paris and gilded with metallic leaf. The original shape to make the mould was achieved by packing clay on to a wooden frame and sculpting it to form the curved surround. (Stirling & Bullus)

Right: this forbidding looking plaster cast frame was inspired by the Gothic style and graveyard sculpture. (Jo Smith)

Right: this scroll-shaped frame is made by covering a chicken wire frame with two or three layers of papier-mâché. When dry, the frame is painted with a coat of white emulsion (latex), and then decorated with brightly coloured papers and gold paint. (Jennie Neame)

MILLEFIORI FRAME

MILLEFIORI LITERALLY MEANS "A THOUSAND FLOWERS". THIS FRAME COMBINES POLYMER CLAY "CANES" TO MAKE KALEIDOSCOPIC PATTERNS.

MATERIALS
— AND —
EQUIPMENT

polymer clay in 4 colours
rolling pin
cutting blade
wooden frame
glass diamanté "gems"
strong glue

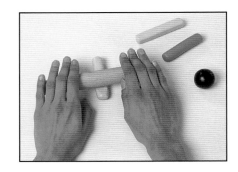

1 Knead the clay so it is easy to work. Roll each colour into a sausage and then square off each sausage by making four lengthways sides with a rolling pin. These square-section rods of clay are called "canes".

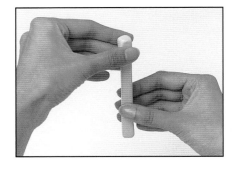

2 Hold a cane in one hand, and, using the thumb and forefinger of the other hand, elongate it by gently smoothing and stretching it downwards. Repeat with each cane, then cut each one into quarters.

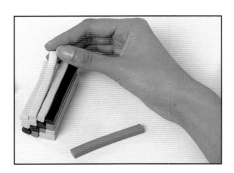

3 Combine the colours in sequence to build up a chequer-board pattern. Gently compress the chequer-board cane. Elongate the cane as in step 2 or by rolling each side evenly with the rolling pin, until it is about 1 cm (½ in) wide. Cut the block in half and trim the ends. Put one half to one side to make petal shapes at a later stage.

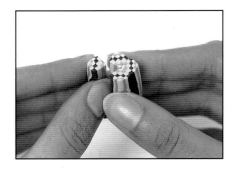

4 Take one half and reduce its width further, to about 4 mm (⅙ in) in width. Check the pattern by trimming the ends. Make sure that the pattern doesn't get so small that it loses clarity. Cut the cane into four equal lengths. Put the four pieces together by matching up the colours. Gently compress the cane to hold it together.

5 Cut thin slices from the cane and press them on to the frame, smoothing the pieces together. Cover the whole frame. Roll the frame gently with the rolling pin to even out the surface. Trim the edges with the blade. Bake at the recommended temperature, according to the manufacturer's instructions on the packet of polymer clay.

6 Make the flower decorations by compressing the remnants of the cane into a petal shape with your fingers. Do the same to the larger cane that you put aside in step 3. This will provide a larger size of petal.

7 Take slices from both sizes of canes and press them on to the frame. Work from the outside of each flower in, making circular layers of petals from the large pattern and the small pattern alternately, to provide contrast. Press the "gems" firmly into the flower centres and then remove them before baking. Small squares of the original chequer-board pattern can also be used as decorative elements between the flowers. Bake the finished frame again. Replace the "gems" and glue them in place.

These exquisite frames are made by rolling different coloured canes of polymer clay together.
(Deborah Alexander)

WAND MIRROR FRAME

A MAGICAL FRAME WHICH USES UP LITTLE ODDS
AND ENDS YOU HAVE LYING ABOUT THE HOUSE.
USE OLD BUTTONS, BEADS, SHELLS AND EVEN KEYS.

MATERIALS
— AND —
EQUIPMENT

copper wire

wire cutters

round-nosed pliers

bits and pieces to decorate, including shells
and glass or plastic nuggets

strong glue

self-hardening clay

rolling pin

plastic sheet

clay-modelling tool

cardboard ring-shape template with an
outer diameter of 18 cm (7 in) and an
inner diameter of 11.5 cm (4½ in)

mirror with a diameter of 9 cm (3½ in)

2 pieces of aluminium tubing,
about 1 cm (½ in) in diameter and
about 20 cm (8 in) long

small plastic drinks (soda) bottle

plaster of Paris

acrylic paints

paintbrushes

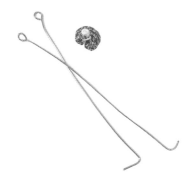

1 Cut the copper wire into different lengths with the cutters. Using the pliers, twist the wire into curling shapes and glue pieces from your assortment on to one end of each wire. Bend the other end of the wires to make a hook shape.

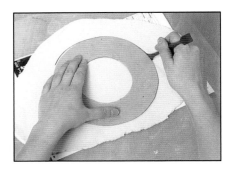

2 Roll out two pieces of clay on the plastic sheet. Using the template and the modelling tool, cut two circles of 18 cm (7 in) diameter, and cut the 11.5 cm (4½ in) circle out of the centre of one large circle. You now have a large circle and a ring of the same diameter.

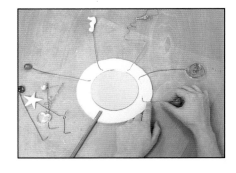

3 Place the mirror in the middle of the circle and arrange the wires round the edge, with the decorated ends outwards. Gently push the hooked ends into the clay. Put one aluminium tube in the position which you want to become the bottom of the mirror frame.

4 Place the clay ring on top and smooth off the overlap round the mirror and the tube with your finger and a little water. Smooth off the sides with the modelling tool. Decorate the front of the frame with small circles of clay. Leave the whole thing to dry – this may take up to two days.

5 To make the base, cut the bottle in half and make four 5 cm (2 in) cuts round the top half of the bottle. Make a hole in the lid.

Mix enough plaster of Paris to half-fill the bottle base and pour it in. Push the top of the bottle part-way into the base and push the second aluminium tube through the hole in the bottle-lid down into the plaster. The top of the bottle will support the tube while the plaster sets round it.

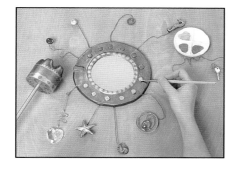

6 When dry remove the plastic from the plaster. Remove the tube and fit the real tube and mirror into the plaster base. Paint the base, stand and frame with acrylic paints.

This frame is made out of two layers of self-hardening clay, into which are embedded pieces of bent copper wire attached to small decorative objects such as can be found lying around the house.
(Ofer Acoo)

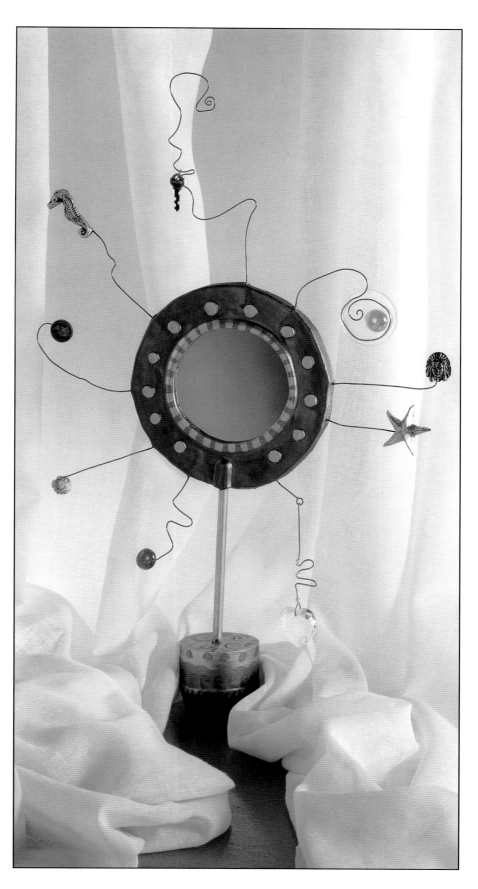

HARLEQUIN PATTERN MIRROR FRAME

A PRETTY FRAME MADE FROM SELF-HARDENING CLAY. THE COLOURS AND DIAMOND SHAPE ARE REMINISCENT OF A HARLEQUIN'S COSTUME.

A mirror made of self-hardening clay, richly painted in harlequin colours. The four corners are embellished with glass nuggets and copper wire. (Ofer Acoo)

MATERIALS
— AND —
EQUIPMENT

copper wire
wire cutters and round-nosed pliers
pencil
tracing paper
scissors
cardboard
rolling pin
self-hardening clay
cutting mat
clay-modelling tool
diamond-shaped mirror
4 glass nuggets
acrylic paints
paintbrushes

1 Cut the wire into four 30 cm (12 in) lengths with the cutters. Twist the wires into shapes with the round-nosed pliers.

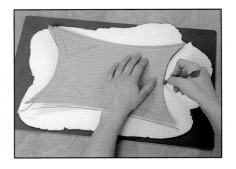

2 Trace the template on page 157 and cut a template out of the cardboard. Roll out the clay to a thickness of about 5 mm (¼ in) and cut it to shape on the cutting mat with the modelling tool. Keep the tool wet all the time you are using it.

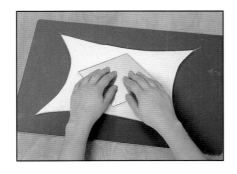

3 Place the mirror on the clay and press down firmly to make a shallow indentation.

4 Remove the mirror. Score a diamond shape 1 cm (½ in) inside the indentation and remove the centre. This hole allows air bubbles to escape from the frame as it drys.

5 Roll out a second piece of clay and cut round the mirror, leaving a 1 cm (½ in) border all the way round. Replace the mirror in the centre of the frame. Place the clay diamond-shape over the mirror.

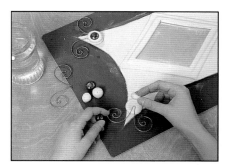

6 Wet your fingers and smooth down the overlap all round the mirror. Seal the edges with the modelling tool, so that the mirror is held securely between two layers of clay. Cut a diamond shape 1 cm (½ in) in from the edges of the mirror and remove the piece of clay from the middle, revealing the mirror.

7 Make eight clay balls and place one in each corner of the frame. Working one corner at a time, press on a ball to flatten it, place a wire on it and push a second ball on top and the glass nugget on top of that. Push hard so all the pieces are firmly attached. Repeat with the other corners.

8 Score a pattern near the corners of the frame. Leave the frame to dry for two or three days and then paint it with acrylic paints.

SALT DOUGH ANGEL FRAME

 SALT DOUGH IS A TRADITIONAL AND INEXPENSIVE MEDIUM FOR THREE-DIMENSIONAL MODELLING. THE DOUGH IS PLIABLE AND EASY TO WORK WITH, AND YOU WILL BE ABLE TO MODEL INTRICATE DETAILS VERY REALISTICALLY. THESE SIMPLE ANGELS HAVE A DELIGHTFUL FOLK-ART LOOK.

MATERIALS
AND
EQUIPMENT

2 cups plain (all-purpose) flour
1 cup salt
about 1 cup water
mixing bowl
metal spoon
airtight container
baking parchment
rolling pin
pencil
tracing paper
small sharp knife
drinking straw
scrap of corrugated cardboard
water-colour paints
paintbrushes
polyurethane satin varnish

MAKING THE SALT DOUGH

1 Mix up the flour, salt and half the water in the bowl.

2 Gradually add more water and knead together for 5 minutes, or until the dough has a smooth, firm consistency. Be careful not to add too much water, or the dough will sag and become sticky.

To make the Angel Frame

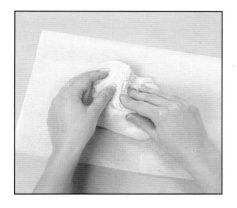

1 Remove the dough from the bowl and knead it for 10 minutes. If possible, leave it to rest for 30 minutes in an airtight container. Preheat the oven to 120°C/250°F/Gas ½.

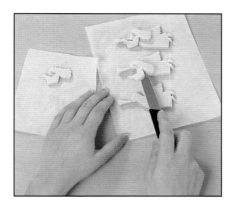

2 On the baking parchment, roll out the dough to 1 cm (½ in) thick. Copy the templates on page 153 and cut out the frame, three angels and three hair and arm shapes from the dough. Place the hair and arm pieces on top of the angels.

3 Mark details with the knife tip on the angels.

4 Roll the remaining dough 5 mm (¼ in) thick. Cut a circle 10.5 cm (4⅛ in) in diameter. Cut a narrow strip 1 cm (½ in) wide. Lay it round half the circumference of the circle. This circle will form the back of the frame.

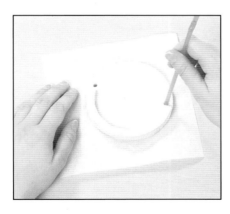

5 Pierce two holes in the circle for hanging, using the straw.

6 Bake the frame and the angels for an hour. Moisten the underside of the angels and smear them with raw dough. Press the angels on to the frame and bake both the frame and the circle for 8 hours.

Continued ▶

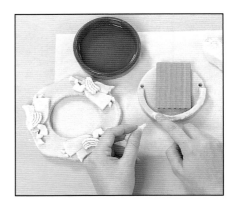

Opposite: a salt dough frame decorated with trumpeting angels. The frame, angels and back of the frame are made in separate sections which are baked individually before being assembled. This can be time consuming and requires a little patience, but the end result is well worth waiting for. (Cheryl Owen)

7 Moisten the top of the semi-circular strip and smear it with raw dough (this will act as a glue when the frame is placed on top of it). Put a scrap of corrugated cardboard at the top of the circle to balance the frame evenly on top. This will create a slit through which to insert your picture. Press the frame on to the backing circle and bake for another 2 hours.

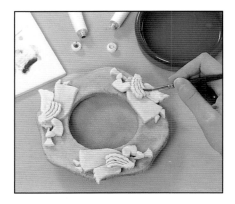

8 Leave to cool and then remove the scrap of cardboard. Paint with water-colour paints. Varnish with five coats of varnish, leaving 4 hours between each coat.

Right: a salt dough frame inspired by the sun. The shape is similar to those used on old sea charts, with alternate wiggly and straight edges to the rays of the sun. (Cheryl Owen)

SPECTACULAR STAR FRAME

A plain frame is decorated with salt dough stars, each painted with patterns, to create a wacky frame. Note the vibrant colours, which are just unusual shades of emulsion (latex) paints. (Petra Boase)

A PLAIN FRAME CAN BE TRANSFORMED BY DECORATING IT WITH BRIGHTLY PAINTED CUT-OUT SHAPES MADE FROM SALT DOUGH.

MATERIALS
— AND —
EQUIPMENT

2 cups plain (all-purpose) flour

1 cup salt

1 cup water

mixing bowl

metal spoon

rolling pin

pencil

tracing paper

chopping board

small sharp knife

baking parchment

fine-grade sandpaper

acrylic gesso

paintbrushes

emulsion (latex) paints in a variety of bright colours

PVA (white) glue

MDF (medium-density fiberboard) frame

satin varnish

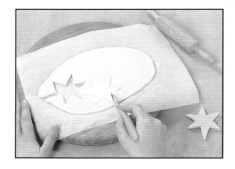

1 Mix the dough as instructed on page 72, knead it for 10 minutes and roll it out. Trace the template on page 153 and follow it to cut out the stars with the knife. Bake the stars for 5 hours at 120°C/250°F/Gas ½.

2 Leave the stars to cool and then sand them with fine sandpaper.

3 Paint each star with gesso and leave to dry. This will give some body to the stars and it is a good surface on which to apply the emulsion (latex) paint. Decorate the stars with a coat of emulsion as a base colour. Leave to dry.

4 Paint patterns in other colours on the stars. Glue the stars on to the frame. Finish with a coat of varnish.

Wood, Glass & Metal Frames

 THERE ARE SOME WONDERFUL, INSPIRATIONAL FRAMES IN OUR GALLERY SECTION, BUT THE PRACTICAL PROJECTS ARE MORE EASILY MADE AND PERHAPS A LITTLE MORE UNUSUAL. THE "WOOD" USED IN MANY OF THE PROJECTS IN THIS BOOK IS IN FACT MDF (MEDIUM-DENSITY FIBERBOARD). I MAKE NO EXCUSE FOR USING THIS, BECAUSE UNLESS THE WOOD IS BEAUTIFUL AND WILL BE SEEN, AN INEXPENSIVE, STRONG ALTERNATIVE IS JUST AS GOOD.

WE HAVE USED GLASS IN THE FORM OF BEADS, AND THE COPPER AND ALUMINIUM FOIL USED IS AVAILABLE IN SHEET FORM FROM WELL-STOCKED CRAFT SHOPS OR METAL SUPPLIERS.

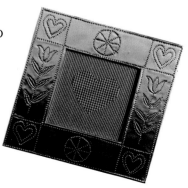

Right: these jewel-like frames are made by soldering unfassetted glass nuggets together. The nuggets on the heart-shaped frame are fixed to the very edge to allow the light to shine through them. (Polly Plouviez)

Left: metal foils are an easy way of decorating a frame as they are soft and malleable. (Helen Musselwhite)

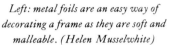

Below: these two wooden frames have a strong seashore feel. They are decorated with shells and glass nuggets, and the distressed paint finishes are reminiscent of worn driftwood. (Rachel Maidens)

Right: inspired by world folk art and Mediterranean colours this wooden frame is decorated with embossed metal foil. (Helen Musselwhite)

Above: the inspiration for these frames comes from the colour effects of verdigris. In complete contrast to the mottled organic quality of the surfaces, the geometric shapes and hard-edged decorative lines provide elements of containment and counterpoint. The frames are made from brass and copper and are decorated using chemical and heat patination techniques. (John McKellar)

CROWN FRAME WITH FOIL SHAPES

A fun frame cut from MDF (medium-density fiberboard), the top of which is cut like a crown and decorated with brightly painted paper baubles (balls). The front face of the frame is decorated with embossed metallic foil shapes. (Petra Boase)

THESE FOIL SHAPES ARE EASILY CUT WITH SCISSORS, AND ARE EMBOSSED BY MARKING WITH A BALLPOINT PEN FROM THE BACK.

MATERIALS
— AND —
EQUIPMENT

pencil

tracing paper

jig-saw

sheet of MDF (medium-density
fiberboard)

pink, green, blue, purple and yellow
emulsion (latex) paint

paintbrushes

5 paper baubles (balls)

5 pencils

florist's foam

tomato purée (paste) tubes, cleaned and
opened out

ballpoint pen

scissors

strong glue

1 Make a template by tracing the one from page 154. Draw round it on the wood and cut out the frame with a jig-saw. Paint it with emulsion (latex), using different colours for the front, back and rebate (rabbet).

2 Push the baubles on to the ends of the pencils and stick the pencils in the florist's foam. Paint each bauble a different colour.

3 Draw flower, star and heart shapes on the back of the opened-out metal tubes, using the ballpoint pen. Draw decorative details on the shapes to form the embossed pattern. Using scissors, carefully cut round the metal shapes.

4 Scatter the shapes on the frame and glue them in position. Glue the painted baubles on to the spikes at the top of the frame.

PUNCHED-METAL FOLK ART FRAME

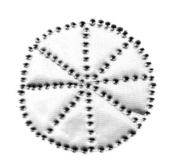

 PUNCHED-METAL WORK IS A COLONIAL CRAFT THAT WAS COMMON IN EARLY-AMERICAN HOMES. THE TECHNIQUE IS NOW UNDERGOING A REVIVAL.

MATERIALS
— AND —
EQUIPMENT

large soft cloth

sheet of thin aluminium foil,
1 cm (½ in) wider all round than the frame

27 cm (10½ in) square softwood frame,
with sides 6.5 cm (2½ in) deep

ballpoint pen

scissors

bradawl (awl)

brass escutcheon pins 1.5 cm (¾ in) and
1 cm (½ in) long, depending on depth of
rebate (rabbet) in frame

tack hammer

white chinagraph pencil (china marker)

soft cloth for cleaning

1 Spread out the cloth and put the sheet of aluminium foil on top. Lay the frame upside-down on the foil and draw round the outer and inner edges with a ballpoint pen. Mark a further inner frame 1.5 cm (¾ in) deep, to allow for turning around the rebate (rabbet) of the frame.

2 Cut out the outer corners of the foil with scissors. Cut out the middle of the foil, carefully following the innermost line. Snip in to the corners of the foil turnings at a 45-degree angle.

3 Bring the foil round the frame and make holes with a bradawl (awl). Bang the longer pins in through the holes, using a tack hammer, all round the outer edges of the frame.

4 Fold the foil round the inside of the frame, mark it with holes and pin it to the rebate with the short pins, as you did the outside.

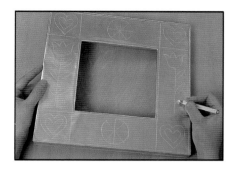

5 Draw lines on the front of the frame with a chinagraph pencil (china marker) and ruler to divide it into squares and rectangles. Draw a heart in each corner and a circle in the top and bottom rectangles with the chinagraph pencil. Add star shapes within the circles and outlines within the hearts. Draw a tulip on both sides of the frame. Freehand drawing helps to keep the naïve look associated with punched-metal work. The outlines are easily cleaned off with a cloth.

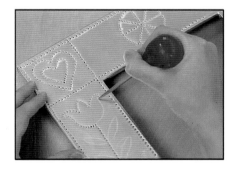

6 Prick all the outlines through the metal and the wood using the bradawl. Wipe off any marks using a slightly soapy soft cloth.

Foil is decorated with naïve motifs, which are made by punching holes in the foil and the wooden frame with a bradawl (awl).
(Deborah Schneebeli-Morrell)

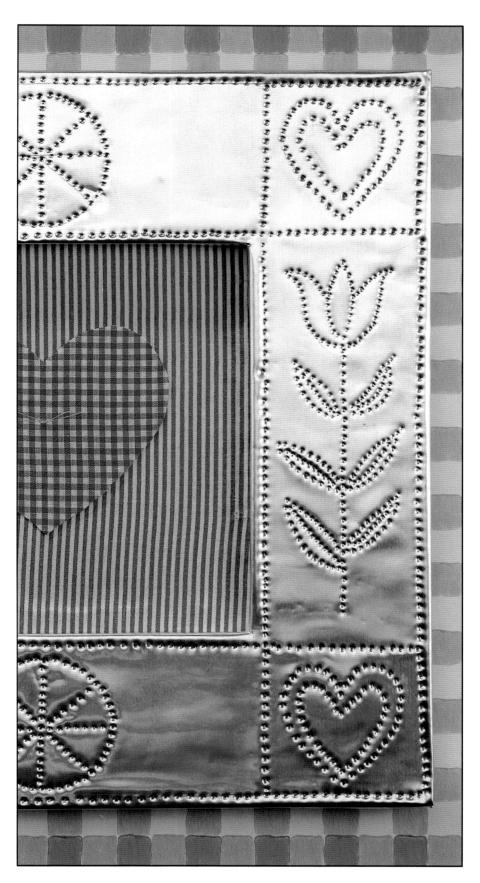

COPPER FRAME WITH EMBOSSED SHAPES

A softwood frame is covered with copper foil and then decorated with embossed aluminium shapes and brass pins. This frame has a very professional look, but the techniques are quite simple.
(Deborah Schneebeli-Morrell)

THIS FRAME COMBINES TWO METAL FOILS TO STUNNING EFFECT. THE EMBOSSED SHAPES AND SIMPLE NAIL PATTERNS ARE VERY STRIKING.

MATERIALS
—— AND ——
EQUIPMENT

large soft cloth

sheet of thin copper foil,
1 cm (½ in) wider than the frame

softwood frame with sides at least
7 cm (2¾ in) deep

ballpoint pen

scissors

bradawl (awl)

brass escutcheon pins 1.5 cm (¾ in)
and 1 cm (½ in), depending on depth of
rebate (rabbet) in frame

tack hammer

sheet of thin aluminium foil

white chinagraph pencil (china marker)

metal polish and soft cloth

1 Spread out the cloth and put the copper foil on it. Lay the frame upside-down on the foil and draw round the outer and inner edges with the ballpoint pen.

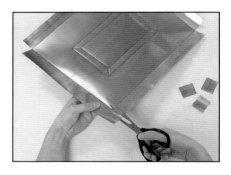

2 Mark an inner frame 1.5 cm (¾ in) deep, to allow for turning around the rebate (rabbet) of the frame. Cut out the outer corners and the middle of the foil with scissors.

3 Fold the foil round the outer edges of the frame and make holes with a bradawl (awl). Hammer the longer pins in through the holes. Fold the foil round the rebate and mark and pin it with the short pins.

4 Draw simple flower and leaf shapes on the back of the aluminium foil with the chinagraph pencil (china marker). Cut out the shapes using scissors.

5 Place the cut-out shapes on the soft cloth and draw decorative patterns on the back of them with the ballpoint pen.

6 Place the flowers and leaves around the frame and prick through both the metals and the wood, using the bradawl. Using the long pins, nail the shapes on to the frame through the pricked holes.

7 Further decorate the frame with more long pins hammered in to form star shapes. Finish off by gently rubbing the whole frame with a soft cloth and metal polish.

BEADWORK FRAME

Inspired by water this frame is made by weaving rocaille beads on a loom. The woven strips are then stuck onto a wooden frame and edged with beading. (Debbie Siniska)

STRIPS OF WOVEN ROCAILLE BEADS (SMALL GLASS SEED BEADS) ARE MOUNTED ON A WOODEN FRAME. FOR THIS PROJECT YOU NEED A SPECIAL BEAD LOOM.

MATERIALS
— AND —
EQUIPMENT

paper for template
ruler
pencil
scissors
flat-faced wooden frame
moulding (cut into mitred lengths to fit the outer and inner edges of the front of the frame)
graph paper
coloured pencils
bead loom
bonded nylon thread
size 11/0 rocaille beads in different colours
beading needle
needle and thread
backing fabric
dressmaker's pins
strong glue
tack hammer
brass panel pins

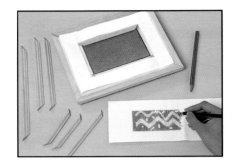

1 Make a paper template the dimensions of the front face of the frame, minus the width of both the inner and outer mouldings. (Remember that the inner moulding has to overlap the picture area in order to hold the glass.) Draw out your design on graph paper, using one square to represent one bead, and a different coloured pencil for each colour of bead.

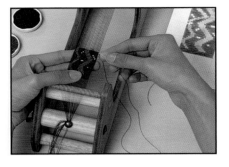

2 Thread the bead loom with the nylon thread according to the manufacturer's instructions. Weave four strips of beadwork to fit the template, following the design on the graph paper.

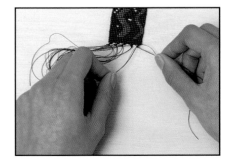

3 Remove each beadwork strip from the loom as you finish it and tie off the warp ends.

4 Fold the warp ends behind the beadwork and oversew the ends of the strip to hold the warp ends firmly in place.

5 Cut out the backing fabric slightly larger than the paper template. Sew the beadwork strips together to form a frame. Pin and then sew them on to the backing fabric.

6 Place the beadwork frame on the front face of the wooden frame and glue it in position.

7 Take the lengths of outer and inner moulding and secure into place with strong glue. Hammer in the panel pins to fix the moulding securely at the ends of each length.

BEADED VELVET FRAME

THE LUXURIOUS TEXTURE AND GLOWING COLOUR OF VELVET IS HIGHLIGHTED WITH THE JEWEL-LIKE COLOURS OF GLASS AND METALLIC BEADS, TO PRODUCE AN EFFECT OF CONSIDERABLE SOPHISTICATION AND STYLE. THE BEADS ARE HELD IN PLACE BY PINS, WHICH CAN JUST BE PUSHED INTO POSITION, SO THIS GLAMOROUS EFFECT IS VERY SIMPLE TO ACHIEVE.

MATERIALS
— AND —
EQUIPMENT

cardboard
pencil
ruler
craft knife
midnight blue velvet square
sharp-pointed scissors
needle and thread
metallic beads
glass beads
pins
self-adhesive felt
PVA (white) glue

1 Cut out a square from the cardboard at least 1 cm (½ in) smaller than the velvet square. Cut out a square from the middle to make a frame. To cover the cardboard frame with velvet, place the velvet right-side down and put the frame on top. On the outside edge, leave a 1 cm (½ in) seam allowance and mitre the corners. Cut away the middle section of velvet leaving a 1 cm (½ in) seam allowance and snipping into the corners.

2 With a needle and thread and using large stitches, pull the sides of the velvet together over the back of the cardboard frame.

A frame covered in velvet is further embellished by sticking pins with beads threaded on to them all round the frame. This is inspired by the techniques of Indian embroidery, in which the use of pins and beads is widespread.
(Isabel Stanley)

3 Thread the beads on to the pins, first a metallic one and then a glass one on each pin. Push the pins firmly into the inside and outside edges of the cardboard.

4 Cut a backing square from the cardboard at least 1 cm (½ in) smaller all round than the finished frame. Cover it on both sides with self-adhesive felt. Glue it on the back of the frame on three sides.

FABRIC FRAMES

 THIS CHAPTER ILLUSTRATES A WIDE VARIETY OF TECHNIQUES FOR MAKING AND COVERING FRAMES, USING MANY DIFFERENT KINDS OF FABRICS AND METHODS. SOMETIMES, THE FABRICS ARE STITCHED, OTHERS ARE GLUED, HOOKED, PAINTED OR CROSS-STITCHED. IF YOU DECIDE YOU LIKE THE IDEA OF A PARTICULAR FRAME BUT DO NOT LIKE THE COLOURS, OR THEY WON'T GO WITH THE COLOUR SCHEME IN THE ROOM YOU HAVE IN MIND, ADAPT THEM TO SUIT.

SOME OF THE FRAMES IN THIS SECTION USE LUXURIOUS FABRICS SUCH AS SILK, VELVET, ORGANZA AND SATIN TO PRODUCE RICH SURROUNDS FOR YOUR FAVOURITE PICTURES. BUT YOU CAN ALSO USE ODD SCRAPS OF FABRIC, OR BRIGHTLY COLOURED FELTS TO MAKE FUN FRAMES THAT REQUIRE MINIMAL SEWING SKILLS.

Above and Opposite: these luxurious-looking mirror frames are made with dupion silk, which is padded and embroidered. The mirrors are hand gilded. (Mark Crowther)

Above: two examples of how appliqué can be used to decorate frames. The one in the foreground is made of layers of fabric, some of which are cut away to reveal the fabric below. (Lorna Moffat)
The frame in the background is machine-embroidered on to shot silk and other rich fabrics such as shot velvet and organzas. A metallic organza is twisted and couched down to create the raised surfaces. (Abigail Mill)

Right: rich silks in subtle colourways and fine stripes are used to create classic frames, suitable for any drawing room or bedroom. (The Mulberry Tree)

Right: fabric has been used in the easiest way possible to decorate these wooden frames. The stylized shapes are simply glued in to position and machine embroidery adds texture and detail. (Rachel McDonnell)

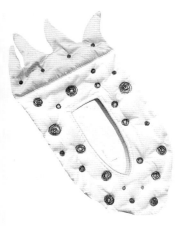

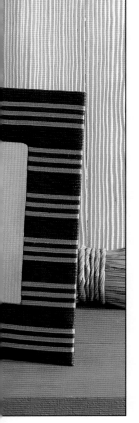

Right: strips of material have been prodded through a hessian (burlap) backing to create this unusual mirror surround. The fabric is shorn using a pair of scissors to give the surface of the frame a pile. (Lizzie Reakes)

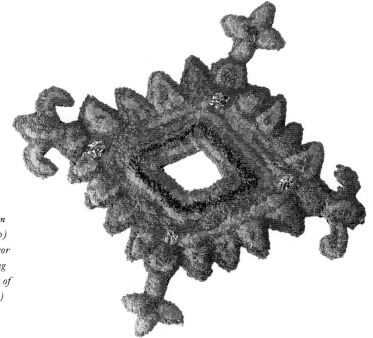

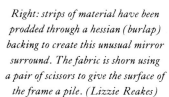

STAR-SHAPED RAG-RUG MIRROR FRAME

 THIS MIRROR FRAME USES THE TECHNIQUE OF HAND-HOOKING WHICH IS A GREAT WAY OF RECYCLING FABRIC SCRAPS.

MATERIALS
— AND —
EQUIPMENT

hessian (burlap)

embroidery hoop

magic marker

hook

1 cm (½ in) wide fabric strips
in assorted colours

latex carpet glue or PVA (white) glue

sharp-pointed scissors

black felt

needle and strong black thread

small mirror

drink-can ring-pull (soda-can pull-tab)

1 Fix the hessian (burlap) in the embroidery hoop and pull it taut. With the magic marker draw a star on the hessian. Leave a 7 cm (3 in) border all the way round between the design and the hoop.

2 Draw a circle in the centre of the star and begin hooking round it. Thread the hook with a fabric strip. Working with one hand under the frame, push the hook through the hessian to the wrong side. Pull the hook back through the hessian, bringing the end of the fabric strip to the right side.

3 This shows the back of the work as it is hooked. Continue hooking, changing colours as appropriate, until all areas are filled.

4 Always bring the ends up from the back to the front of the work and trim them to the same height as the loops.

*A rag-rug technique is used here to create
a mirror or picture frame. A pocket is
sewn on to the back of the frame, in
which a mirror or a picture can be held
in place. (Lizzie Reakes)*

5 Remove the hessian from the frame and lay the work face-down on a flat surface. Cut around the shape, allowing for a border. Apply a thin layer of latex glue all over the reverse, covering the inner circle as well. Leave for about 3–5 minutes, and then fold in the edges and press down firmly to secure them. Cut the inner circle and fold the edges back to reveal the mirror area. Allow the frame to dry for 2 hours.

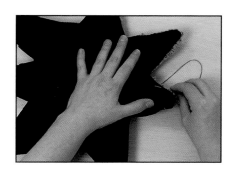

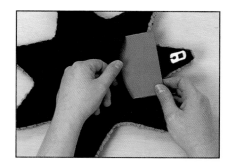

6 Cut out a backing shape from black felt, allowing for turnings. Apply a thin layer of latex glue on the reverse side of the frame. Attach the backing, turning in the edges, and slip-stitch it in place round the edges, using a black thread.

7 Cut through the centre of the felt to reveal the mirror area.

8 Using the mirror as a template, cut a piece of black felt to make a pocket. Pin it in to position in the centre of the back of the frame and blanket-stitch it, using a strong thread. Attach the ring-pull (pull-tab) by sewing it in position.

BAROQUE QUILTED PICTURE FRAME

 THE USE OF LUXURIOUS FABRICS, SUCH AS METALLIC ORGANZA AND RICH VELVET, EMBROIDERED WITH METALLIC THREAD, GIVE THIS FRAME A SUMPTUOUS LOOK THAT IS BELIED BY HOW SIMPLE IT IS TO MAKE.

MATERIALS
—— AND ——
EQUIPMENT

pencil

tissue paper

24 × 24 cm (9½ × 9½ in) piece of velvet

24 × 24 cm (9½ × 9½ in) piece of metallic organza

needle and tacking (basting) thread

old-gold embroidery thread

sewing machine

sharp-pointed scissors

ruler

craft knife

two 15 × 20 cm (6 × 8 in) pieces of cardboard

wadding (batting)

strong glue

self-adhesive black felt

1 Trace the design on page 153 on to tissue paper.

2 Lay the organza and tracing on the velvet and tack together.

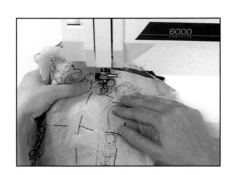

3 Using old-gold thread, machine-stitch the lines of the pattern.

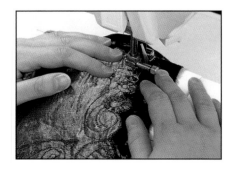

4 Tear away the tissue paper. Fill in the flower shapes and detail using straight machine stitch. Cut away the waste organza from the centre and zig-zag stitch to neaten the edges of the centre of the frame.

A rich machine-embroidered and cut-away appliqué frame worked in organza and silk using metallic thread. (Isabel Stanley)

5 On one piece of cardboard, draw a central rectangle so that you will have a frame with 3.5 cm (1½ in) wide sides. Cut out the centre. (The second piece of cardboard will form the backing.) Cut two layers of wadding (batting) the same size and shape as the frame and glue them both to the frame.

6 Place the cardboard frame on the back of the embroidery, with the wadding on the underside. Cut away the middle section of velvet, leaving a 1 cm (½ in) seam allowance. Snip into the corners. On the outside edge, trim the velvet to leave a 1 cm (½ in) seam allowance and mitre the corners.

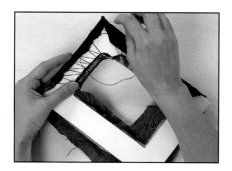

7 Fold the edges over. Pull the fabric over the card frame and sew it together using large stitches.

8 Cover the backing with self-adhesive felt. Fold over the edges and mitre the corners. Glue the two side edges and bottom edge of the backing and place it on the back of the frame. Press flat.

BUCKRAM FRAME

A frame made from a very humble material, buckram, which has been pleated and sewn on to a card base to surround a mirror. (Karen Triffitt)

 BUCKRAM IS COARSE, STIFFENED LINEN AND IS AVAILABLE FROM MILLINERY SUPPLIERS.

MATERIALS
— AND —
EQUIPMENT

pair of compasses
pencil
heavy cardboard
scissors
hole punch
cord
PVA (white) glue
28 cm (11 in) diameter mirror
1 m (1 yard) white cotton fabric
iron
strong clear glue for sticking fabric on to mirror
needle and black and white thread
tissue paper
1 m (1 yard) buckram
30 cm (12 in) black silk organza
sewing machine
acrylic varnish
dressmaker's pins

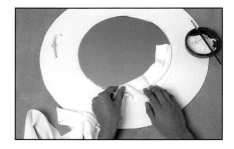

1 Cut a circle from the heavy cardboard with a 50 cm (20 in) diameter. Punch two holes in the cardboard circle and thread the cord through them. Knot the cord at the front and glue it down. Glue the mirror in the centre of the cardboard. Cut a 7 cm (2¾ in) wide strip of white cotton on the bias. Fold over a 2.5 cm (1 in) turning along one long side and iron flat. Open out the fold and glue the turning round the edge of the mirror with strong clear glue, easing it to fit the curve. The fold should be facing inwards and should slightly overlap the edge of the mirror. Fold back the strip and glue it down, on top of the turning, all round.

2 Cut two rings from the cotton. One should have an outer diameter of 55 cm (22 in) and an inner diameter of 26 cm (10¼ in). The other should have an outer diameter of 40 cm (16 in) and an inner diameter of 25.5 cm (10 in). Sew together around the inner edge and trim the seam. Fold the material back so the seam is on the inside and iron flat.

3 Glue the smaller circle on to the cardboard round the mirror. Smooth out the larger circle, fold the overlap over the cardboard and glue it down on the back all round. Cut a backing circle of cotton the same diameter as the cardboard and cut a slit in it for the cord. Glue on to the cardboard and pull the cord through.

4 Make tissue paper patterns from the three templates on page 155 and use them to cut out the buckram shapes. Cut large triangles from the black organza and hand-stitch them in place on each buckram piece using black thread.

5 Cut strips of the organza and arrange them in stripes on top of the triangles. Machine-stitch them into place using black thread. Then blanket-stitch in white thread around the edge of each buckram piece. Rows of white zig-zag stitch can then be sewn between the organza strips. Pleat each buckram piece, varnish them and leave to dry.

6 Arrange the pieces of buckram on the frame base. Each piece should only need three or four pins to keep it in place (one at each end and one or two in between). Overlap the pieces to produce a pleasing shape round the mirror. Stitch the pieces of buckram on to the fabric behind wherever the pins are.

FELT COLLAGE FRAME

Brightly coloured felts in wacky patterns are used to decorate an unusual shaped MDF (medium-density fiberboard) frame. The shapes are simply stuck in to position with glue. (Petra Boase)

FELT IS A GREAT MATERIAL BECAUSE IT DOESN'T FRAY WHEN CUT AND IT CAN BE EITHER SEWN OR GLUED IN PLACE. IT COMES IN VIVID COLOURS, SO IT'S IDEAL FOR A BRIGHT, MODERN INTERIOR. YOU CAN COPY THE FLUID OUTLINE OF THE FRAME SHOWN HERE OR EXPERIMENT WITH YOUR OWN DESIGNS.

MATERIALS
—— AND ——
EQUIPMENT

pencil

paper

scissors

MDF (medium-density fiberboard)

jig-saw

emulsion (latex) paint

paintbrush

felt sheets in selection of colours

ballpoint pen

fabric glue

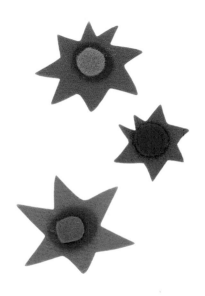

1 Trace your chosen design on to the wood and cut out the frame with a jig-saw. Paint it with emulsion (latex) and leave to dry. Place the frame on a sheet of felt and draw round the edge with the pen.

2 Snip the centre diagonally, and cut out the felt. Glue the piece of felt on to the front of the frame. Glue the centre flaps back, over the rebate (rabbet) on to the back of the frame.

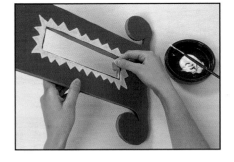

3 Cut out a zig-zag felt border and stick this on to the inner edge of the frame. Glue narrow strips of felt in a contrasting colour around the rebate of the frame.

4 Cut out the felt shapes for decoration and stick them all over the frame.

CROSS-STITCH FRAME

CROSS-STITCH IS A POPULAR CRAFT; ONE WHICH CREATES A CHARMING EFFECT WITH LITTLE EFFORT. ONCE THE BASIC TECHNIQUE HAS BEEN MASTERED, IT'S VERY SIMPLE TO DO. THIS FRAME IS MADE BY MOUNTING THE CROSS-STITCH DESIGN ON A CARDBOARD FRAME.

MATERIALS
— AND —
EQUIPMENT

ruler

pencil

11-count cream cross-stitch fabric

sewing needle

tacking (basting) thread in a
contrasting colour

embroidery hoop

2 skeins each of gold, light green and
forest green stranded cotton

size 26 tapestry needle

iron

cardboard

craft knife

scissors

dressmaker's pins

fabric glue

1 Refer to the chart on page 152. Mark the centre and the position of the frame on the canvas by making large tacking (basting) stitches.

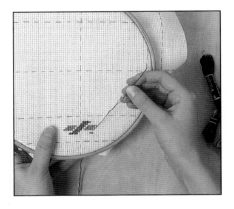

2 Hold the canvas taut in an embroidery hoop and move the hoop as you work each area of the design. Starting at the centre of one of the long sides of the frame, begin working the design using three strands of cotton. Follow the chart, remembering that each coloured square represents one cross stitch worked over one woven block in the fabric. When the design is finished, iron it flat on the wrong side, over a padded surface such as a towel.

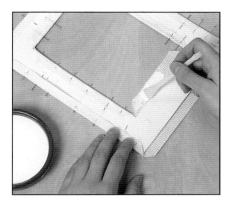

3 Cut a piece of cardboard to the same dimensions as the cross-stitch frame. Cut out the canvas frame, leaving a 1 cm (½ in) border on both the inside and the outside of the frame. Mitre all the corners and then pin and glue the fabric on to the cardboard frame.

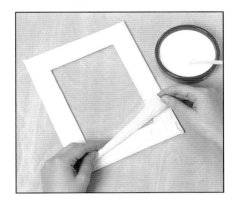

4 When the glue is dry, remove the pins. Cover the back with another frame of cardboard to neaten and strengthen it. Make a backing for the frame by sticking down a plain piece of cardboard on three sides, leaving an opening at the top to allow for a picture to be inserted.

Cross-stitch, although a simple technique, can look very sophisticated, as the rope design round this frame illustrates. The gold and green colours of the stitches are perfect for the picture they surround. (Esther Burt)

PADDED SATIN FRAME

USING WADDING AND RICH FABRICS YOU CAN
CREATE AN ELEGANT MIRROR FRAME. DECORATE
IT WITH EMBROIDERY AND GOLD PAINT.

MATERIALS
—— AND ——
EQUIPMENT

pencil

paper

ruler

scissors

30 × 39 cm (12 × 15½ in) heavy
cardboard

34 × 43 cm (13¾ × 17 in) calico,
for the back

30 × 39 cm (12 × 15½ in) foam card
(foam-core board), 3 mm (¼ in) thick

42 × 51 cm (16¾ × 20½ in) acetate or
silk satin

38 × 47 cm (15 × 18½ in) calico,
for the front

30 × 39 cm (12 × 15½ in) double-sided
fusible buckram

PVA (white) glue

hole punch

20 cm (8 in) nylon cord

18 × 27 cm (7 × 10½ in) mirror

dressmaker's pins

wadding (batting)

iron

Fray-check

paintbrush

gold fabric paint

needle

gold lurex thread

strong glue

1 Trace the template on page 154
and cut out all the elements for
the frame: the cardboard and calico
backing; the foam card (foam-core
board), satin, calico and buckram
frames. Divide the foam card frame in
to two L-shapes. Stick one on to the
backing cardboard. Punch two holes,
thread the hanging cord through, tie it
and glue it down. Glue the mirror in
place and the second L-shape around it.

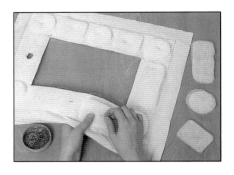

2 Pin the buckram and calico
frames together. Cut a hole
exactly where the knot in the hanging
cord will be. Cut out circles and
rectangles from the wadding (batting)
and pin them on to the buckram.

3 Place the satin frame on an
ironing board face down, and lay
the buckram/calico frame on top, with
the calico facing upwards. Iron all the
inner edges.

4 Turn the material over and iron
from the inside out. This will
fuse the wadding shapes to the
buckram. Use the tip of the iron to
define the shapes.

These frames have been made from fabric which has been padded and stitched to make three-dimensional shapes. The smaller frame is embellished with wire. (Karen Triffitt)

7 Stick the fabric frame on to the foam card frame. Use strong, clear glue for the 1 cm (½ in) overlap around the mirror and PVA (white) glue on the rest. Turn the calico overlap over to the back of the cardboard and stick it down. Repeat with the satin. Trim the top edges to fit above the hanging cord. Stick down a hem of 7 mm (⅓ in) on the calico backing piece. Cut a slit for the hanging cord to pass through. Glue the calico on to the back of the cardboard. Another piece of calico can be glued over the slit to neaten it. A fancy brass picture hook would be a good fixture to hang this mirror frame from. It would complement the gold paint and lurex thread embroidery.

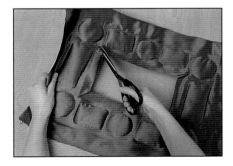

5 Turn the wrong side up again. Use Fray-check on each inner corner, and then snip as far as the edge of the calico. Then glue these flaps over on to the calico.

6 Turn the frame to the right side. Paint the spiral design on the satin using fabric paint. When the paint is dry, embroider textural stitches using gold lurex thread.

PAINTED SILK FRAME

The designer has taken the theme of arches, another form of decorative surround, and used it to create a beautiful frame for this Indian miniature print. (Sarbjit Natt)

THE DESIGN ON THE SILK IS OUTLINED WITH METALLIC GUTTA WHICH ACTS AS A BARRIER TO THE PAINT. THE FINAL EFFECT IS SIMILAR TO THAT OF A STAINED GLASS WINDOW.

MATERIALS
— AND —
EQUIPMENT

drawing paper

selection of coloured pencils

tracing paper

black felt-tipped pen

heavy-weight habotai silk

wooden frame

silk pins or fine map pins

vanishing textile marker

masking tape

metallic gutta and applicator

silk paints in a variety of colours

paintbrushes

paper tissue

2 sheets of clean white paper

iron

scissors

spray adhesive

cardboard

1 Sketch your design and work out the colours to co-ordinate with the picture to be framed. Then draw your final design on to tracing paper with the black pen.

2 Wash, dry and iron the silk. Stretch it on to the wooden frame and hold it in position with the pins. The fabric must be absolutely taut, without any wrinkles.

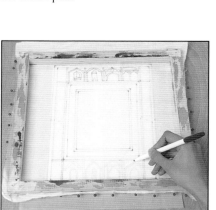

3 Using the vanishing marker, trace the design on to the underside of the stretched silk, holding the tracing paper on the other side with pieces of masking tape at each corner.

4 Apply the metallic gutta to the outline of the design. This will block the mesh of the silk, preventing the silk paints from bleeding and merging. Allow the gutta to dry.

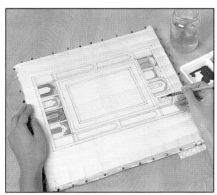

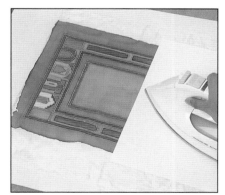

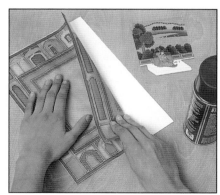

5 Following your initial sketch apply the silk paints, taking care not to splash or go over any lines of gutta. Keep a tissue to hand to mop up any excess paint from your brush. Leave to dry.

6 Place the silk between two sheets of clean white paper and iron it, according to the paint manufacturer's instructions, to fix the paint.

7 Cut neatly around the silk design. The gutta border will prevent the silk from fraying. Use spray adhesive to mount the silk on to the cardboard, cut to the correct size, and stick your picture in the centre.

NATURAL FRAMES

THE USE OF NATURAL MATERIALS IS ECONOMICALLY AND ENVIRONMENTALLY SOUND. YOU CAN CREATE WONDERFUL FRAMES FROM NATURAL MATERIALS THAT CAN BE COLLECTED DURING ANY WOODLAND OR SEASIDE WALK. WE HAVE USED PEBBLES AND DRIFTWOOD THAT HAVE BEEN SMOOTHED BY THE WAVES OVER TIME; DRIED AUTUMNAL LEAVES RICH IN COLOUR; ROPE TWISTED IN TO ATTRACTIVE SHAPES AND THEN NAILED IN PLACE. BUT PERHAPS THE MOST SPECTACULAR FRAME IN THIS SECTION IS MADE UP OF A HOST OF WOODLAND MEMENTOES, RANGING FROM DRIED MUSHROOMS AND BUNDLES OF TWIGS TO FIR CONES, SURROUNDED BY SOFT GREEN MOSS. YOU COULD MAKE A SIMILAR FRAME USING DRIED FLOWERS INSTEAD, TO PRODUCE AN ATTRACTIVE FLORAL FRAME.

Below: this frame is made from re-cycled wood described by its maker as "urban driftwood". It looks deceptively simple, and yet it is the fine balance of one piece of wood against another which make this a beautiful and covetable piece of work. (Jason Cleverly)

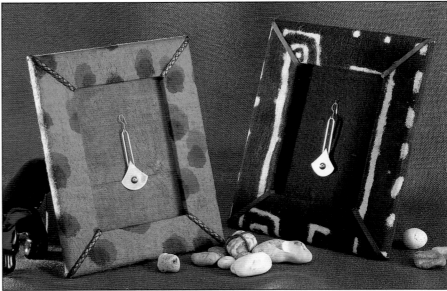

Right: the frame on the left is covered with bark cloth with a leopard skin pattern. On the right, the black and white design is created using mud as a resist while the cloth is dyed. Once the dye is dry, the mud is removed to reveal the original colour below. (Tribal Eye)

Below: wood is easy to decorate with animal patterns; they can be burned in to the wood or painted on. Continuing the theme across a set of frames means that they look good when hung or grouped together. (Tribal Eye)

Above: natural frames can be composed of images and patterns from nature, or they can be made from natural materials, or a combination of both. These frames are made from soap stone which is soft and easily sculpted. One is a zebra skin pattern in black and white, and the other has the carved head of a giraffe in relief and a leaf design down the sides. (Tribal Eye)

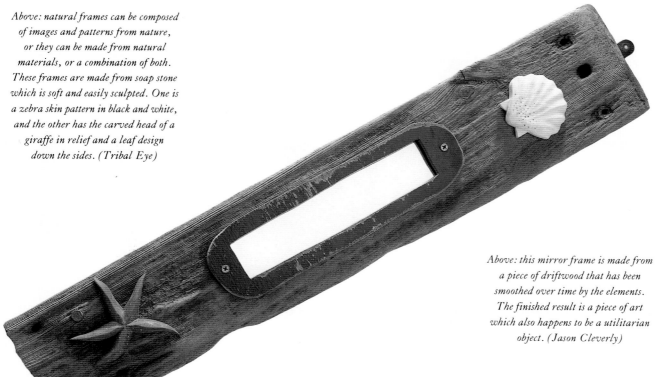

Above: this mirror frame is made from a piece of driftwood that has been smoothed over time by the elements. The finished result is a piece of art which also happens to be a utilitarian object. (Jason Cleverly)

PEBBLE FRAME

THE MATERIALS FOR THIS FRAME COST VERY LITTLE AND IT IS AN IDEAL OPPORTUNITY TO USE UP ALL THOSE STONES YOU COLLECT ON WALKS. TRY TO COLLECT PEBBLES OF AN EVEN SIZE, TO MAKE A SMOOTHER LOOKING FRAME.

A layer of sea-washed pebbles has been embedded in builder's mortar set on a MDF (medium-density fiberboard) frame. Choose pebbles of roughly the same size to make this frame.
(Petra Boase)

MATERIALS
— AND —
EQUIPMENT

MDF (medium-density fiberboard) frame
cream emulsion (latex) paint
paintbrush
grout or mortar
small trowel
small pebbles

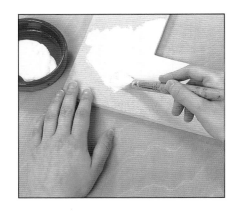

1 Paint the frame with two coats of emulsion (latex). Allow the paint to dry thoroughly before applying the second coat.

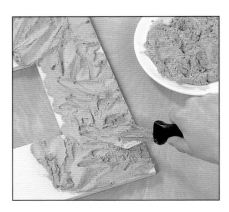

2 Apply grout or mortar to the main body of the frame, a small section at a time, using the trowel.

3 Embed some pebbles in the section of grout or mortar you have applied to the frame before it begins to dry out.

4 Cover the rest of the frame with pebbles in the same way. Smooth more grout or mortar between the pebbles to secure them firmly.

WOODLAND FRAME

Any selection of woody materials can be used to create this woodland-floor look. If the sphagnum moss is very damp, prepare the wire and moss frame and leave to dry for a few days before adding the decorative items.

THIS IS A FAIRLY ADVENTUROUS PROJECT, BUT IF YOU HAVE TIME TO SPARE AND LOTS OF SPACE TO MAKE A MESS, IT IS WELL WORTH THE EFFORT.

MATERIALS
— AND —
EQUIPMENT

chicken wire
strong wire cutters
sphagnum moss
stub (floral) wires
staple gun
substantial wooden frame
mirror
small terracotta flower pots
preserved leaves
twigs and small branches
glue gun
fir cones
dried mushrooms
mossing pins
dark green wood moss

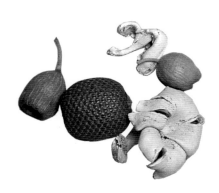

1 Cut four lengths of chicken wire to match the four sides of the frame. The width of each strip of wire needs to be such that, when rolled into a sausage shape, it will cover the face of the frame. Fill the whole length of the chicken wire along the centre with the sphagnum moss, keeping the moss as even as possible.

2 Fold the edges of the chicken wire over to make sausage shapes and "sew" them together every 5–8 cm (2–3 in) with stub (floral) wires.

3 Using a staple gun, fix the moss and chicken wire sausages to the wooden frame. Make sure that each staple covers a piece of wire at each fixing. Repeat this process at 10 cm (4 in) intervals along the edge of the frame and along the sides.

4 Wire the terracotta pots to the frame at random angles by passing a stub wire through the drainage hole and over the pot; twist the two ends together.

5 Make small bunches of the preserved leaves, and, using the stub wires twisted around the stems, push the bunches into the moss base. Work all around the frame, adding the leaves and branches and leaving spaces for the other materials.

6 Using the glue gun, add the cones, mushrooms and other woody items. Make sure that the materials are glued to the moss and the wire frame. Alternatively, wire all the materials and then firmly push the wires into the moss.

7 Using the mossing pins, fill all the small spaces with the green wood moss.

ROPE FRAME

ROPE CAN BE COILED AND NAILED ON TO A
WOODEN FRAME TO CREATE A FRESH, NATURAL
LOOK TO COMPLEMENT ANY INTERIOR.

MATERIALS
—— AND ——
EQUIPMENT

small saw

ruler

90 cm (36 in) of 20 × 10 mm
(¾ × ½ in) wood

sandpaper

four 3 cm (1½ in) panel pins

tack hammer

wood glue

6 m (6½ yards) 5 mm (¼ in) thick rope

about 100 copper hardboard pins (brads)

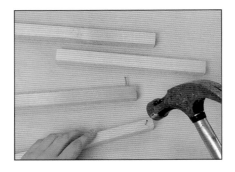

1 Cut the wood into four pieces
each 23 cm (9 in) long. Sand the
rough edges. Hammer in panel pins
1 cm (½ in) from the ends of two of
the pieces of wood, on the narrow
side. These pieces will be the top and
bottom of the frame.

2 Join the sides to the top of the
frame. Stand one side piece on
end. Cover the cut end with wood
glue. Line up the top of the frame
with the side edges. Nail the panel pin
in, so both pieces join. Repeat with
opposite side. Join the bottom of the
frame in the same way.

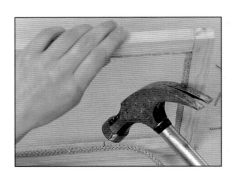

3 Cut an 80 cm (32 in) length of
rope. Spread a thin line of wood
glue on the inside of the frame. Lay
the rope on the glue, keeping it flush
with the front edge of the frame. Fix
the rope in place using hardboard pins
(brads), spacing them about 3 cm
(1½ in) apart.

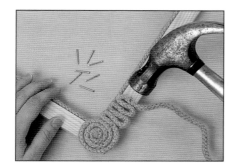

4 Decorate the top of the frame as follows: cut four pieces of rope each measuring 1.25 m (50 in). Starting in one corner, coil a tight spiral of rope measuring about 5 cm (2 in) in diameter. Fix the coil to the corner of the frame with glue and hardboard pins. Continue along the frame towards the next corner, pleating the rope tightly and nailing down every other pleat with hardboard pins. Finish with a tight spiral at the corner, fixed in the same way as the first spiral. Repeat on the bottom of the frame.

For each side, pleat a length of rope in the same way without the spirals. Conceal the ends of the rope by gluing and pinning them to the outside edges of the frame, behind the rope spirals.

Lengths of rope are twisted to form zig-zag patterns and then nailed in to place to decorate the frame. The corners are finished off using coils of rope. Ideal for framing a nautical picture. (Rachel Howard Marshall)

DRIFTWOOD FRAME

THIS FRAME CAN BE MADE FROM ANY BEACH FINDS. WOOD WHICH HAS BEEN SMOOTHED AND WEATHERED BY THE SEA IS BEST. ADD SHELLS OR THE ODD PEBBLE FOR VARIETY. A SEASCAPE PICTURE IS IDEAL FOR A DRIFTWOOD FRAME.

Top left: the frame is made by simply binding shells to lolly (popsicle) sticks at the corner with raffia, creating an Oxford frame. (Lucinda Ganderton) Below: a wooden frame is covered in driftwood and a smoothed piece of glass, and topped with a toy fishing boat. (Petra Boase)

MATERIALS
— AND —
EQUIPMENT

flat-faced wooden frame
deep and pale blue emulsion (latex) paint
paintbrush
wax furniture polish
cloth
fine-grade sandpaper
selection of driftwood
strong glue
shells and/or other finds from the beach
short piece of old rope
small toy boat

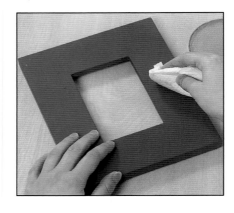

1 Give the frame a base coat of deep blue emulsion (latex) paint. Leave to dry and then rub on a layer of wax polish. Leave to dry.

2 Paint on two coats of pale blue emulsion; leave to dry between coats. Sand away the top coat to reveal the base colour in places.

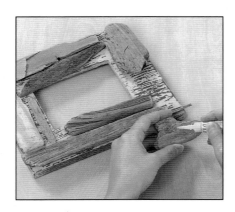

3 Arrange the driftwood pieces on the frame to judge how best to position them. Glue them into place. Add any shells or other bits and pieces that you have.

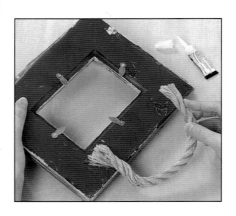

4 Glue the length of rope on to the back of the frame; this will be your hanging hook.

5 Glue the toy boat on to the top of the frame.

Pressed-leaf Frame

THIS FRAME HAS A WARM, AUTUMNAL FEEL

ABOUT IT, AND WOULD MAKE A NOSTALGIC

SOUVENIR OF A MEMORABLE WOODLAND WALK.

Pressed leaves in a variety of autumnal shades have been used to create this nostalgic frame which holds an old sepia photograph. To add to the aged feel of the frame, a layer of crackle varnish is added.
(Lucinda Ganderton)

MATERIALS
—— AND ——
EQUIPMENT

selection of small and medium-size leaves
in various colours

flower press or heavy book

kitchen paper (paper towels)

wooden frame with a wide, flat moulding

PVA (white) glue

crackle glaze

paintbrush

raw umber oil paint

soft cloth

1 Collect a selection of small leaves, looking out for unusual colours and shapes. Make sure that they are dry, and then place them between layers of kitchen paper (paper towels) in a flower press, or between the pages of a heavy book. Leave for at least a week to dry completely.

2 Glue the leaves on to the frame with the PVA (white) glue, coating them one at a time with a thin layer of glue and waiting for it to be partly dry before sticking the leaf down. Begin by arranging a row of overlapping leaves around the outer edge of the frame.

3 Make a second round, using a different kind of leaf. Select four large individual leaves for the corners. Fill in any gaps with the smallest leaves. When the frame is completely covered, paint a thin layer of PVA glue over the whole surface and allow to dry thoroughly.

4 Paint the frame with crackle glaze, following the manufacturer's instructions carefully. When the cracks appear (which may take a while), rub a small amount of raw umber oil paint into the surface of the glaze with a soft cloth, to emphasize the antique effect.

NOVELTY FRAMES

THIS CHAPTER SHOWS WHAT HAPPENS WHEN THE IMAGINATION RUNS RIOT. A FRAME CAN BE MADE FROM ALMOST ANYTHING, OR AT LEAST DECORATED WITH ANYTHING. THESE FRAMES INCLUDE A BROWN-PAPER PARCEL TIED WITH STRING AND SEALING WAX, AND DECORATED WITH STAMPS: A GREAT FRAME FOR A PICTURE POSTCARD OR HOLIDAY SNAP. ON A SEASONAL NOTE, A FRAME IS COVERED WITH TINSEL AND CHRISTMAS DECORATIONS – THIS IS A USEFUL WAY OF USING UP ALL THOSE DECORATIONS WHICH HAVE LOST THEIR STRINGS AND CAN'T BE HUNG ON THE TREE. THESE ARE JUST SOME OF THE IDEAS INCLUDED IN THIS CHAPTER. FOLLOW THE PROJECTS OR EXPERIMENT WITH YOUR OWN IDEAS, BUT DON'T FORGET TO LOOK AT THE GALLERY SECTION FOR FURTHER INSPIRATION.

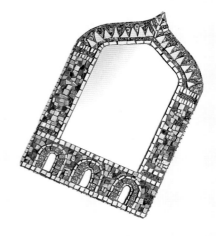

Left: three small mirror frames. Far left, pulped papier-mâché frame. (Sue Sanders) Right, heart-shaped frame with shooting stars. (Rob Turner) Bottom, a hand mirror made from papier-mâché and decorated with flowers and glass nuggets. (Rob Turner)

Above: this mosaic frame is made from a mixture of mosaic tiles and broken pieces of china. The artist draws her influence from Islamic architecture and Indian textiles. (Cleo Mussie)

Above: jester's crown frame. Made in metal the points of the crown are topped with gold baubles. (Bombay Duck)

Above: these brightly coloured, highly ornate and unusual frames are sculpted from self-hardening clay and painted with acrylic paints. Glass nuggets and copper wire bent into wonderful shapes add extra colour and texture.
(Ofer Acoo)

Opposite: wall plaque made from layered papier-mâché. The centre of the plaque and the frame itself are designed as one piece of work.
(Hannah Downes)

BROWN-PAPER PARCEL PICTURE FRAME

Sealing wax, brown paper and string are the chief components of this frame, which is made from folded cardboard. To add colour, collect exotic stamps and stick them on to the frame.
(Lucinda Ganderton)

THIS PROJECT USES EVERYDAY MATERIALS TO MAKE AN UNUSUAL FRAME FOR A POSTCARD FROM AN EXOTIC HOLIDAY. VARIATIONS ON THIS THEME INCLUDE CHRISTMAS WRAPPING PAPER FRAMING A FAMILY SNAPSHOT, OR BIRTHDAY PAPER FOR A PICTURE OF A PARTY.

MATERIALS
— AND —
EQUIPMENT

pencil
tracing paper
cardboard
scissors
ruler
craft knife
cutting mat
sticky tape
brown paper
spray adhesive
string
sealing wax
stamps and stickers

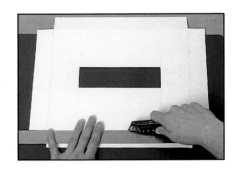

1 Trace the template from page 156 on to the cardboard and cut it out. Using a craft knife and resting on a cutting mat, cut and score down the lines of the cardboard as marked on the template. Remove the narrow central panel. Bend the outer flaps upwards and secure the corners with sticky tape.

2 Cut a piece of brown paper 2.5 cm (1 in) larger all round than the cardboard; you may need to iron the paper, if it has been folded. Spray it lightly with adhesive and place the frame, face-down, centrally on it. Mitre the corners of the brown paper and fold it over the outer edges of the cardboard. Trim the overlap and secure it with sticky tape on the back of the frame.

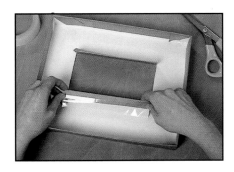

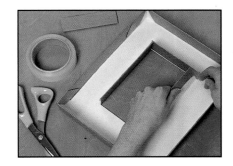

3 From the back of the frame, cut through the brown paper along the short edges of the inner rectangle and down the centre of the gap. Bend back the two inner flaps of cardboard so they stand upright, fold back the brown paper to cover the flaps and stick it down.

4 Cut two lengths of cardboard the same length as the short edge of the inner rectangle and 4 cm (1½ in) wide. Cover them with brown paper and secure them in position with sticky tape on the short sides of the inner rectangle, from the inside of the frame.

5 Tie a short length of string around the centre of each side of the frame, and then wrap a longer length around the outer edge, tying a bow in the top. Drip sealing wax on to the string in a few places. Decorate the parcel with overseas stamps. Stick the picture in place with tape.

CHRISTMAS FRAME WITH WOODEN FIGURES

Tinsel and decorative wooden figures have been used imaginatively to make Christmas frames. They are inexpensive to make and are ideal festive gifts.
(Oliver Moxley)

THIS FRAME IS MADE BY USING CHRISTMAS TREE DECORATIONS AND TINSEL TO EMBELLISH A PLAIN WOODEN FRAME. IT IS IDEAL FOR CHILDREN TO MAKE IN THE EXCITING RUN-UP TO CHRISTMAS, AS WELL AS A GOOD WAY OF USING UP SPARE OR SLIGHTLY DAMAGED ORNAMENTS.

MATERIALS
— AND —
EQUIPMENT

flat-faced wooden frame
gold paint or spray paint
paintbrush
glue gun
red and silver tinsel
scissors
small wooden Christmas tree decorations

1 Paint the frame with gold paint or spray it with a gold spray paint. Leave to dry.

2 Glue the red tinsel round the face of the frame.

3 Glue the silver tinsel over the frame on top of the red tinsel.

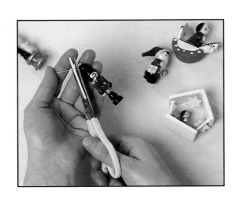

4 Cut any strings off the wooden tree decorations.

5 Arrange the wooden figures around the frame and glue them in place.

SPARKLING CABOCHONS & GOLD FRAME

These sparkling frames are made by simply covering the frame in decorator's filler (spackle), in to which the plastic cabochons are set. When dry, the filler is painted gold. (Jack Moxley)

A HUMBLE FRAME CAN BE GIVEN A NEW LEASE OF LIFE WITH PLASTIC CABOCHONS, SEQUINS OR DIAMANTÉ, EMBEDDED IN DECORATOR'S FILLER (SPACKLE). CABOCHONS ARE POLISHED BUT UNCUT STONES, OR STONES CUT ROUND, WITHOUT FACETS.

MATERIALS
— AND —
EQUIPMENT

sandpaper
frame
decorator's filler (spackle)
knife
plastic cabochons, sequins or diamanté
gold acrylic paint
paintbrush

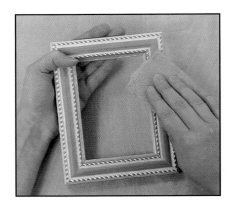

1 Sand the frame to create a rough surface on which to apply the decorator's filler (spackle).

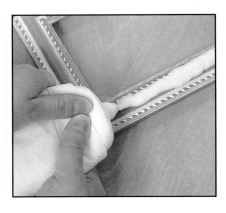

2 Squeeze the filler out of the tube on to the frame.

3 Texture the surface of the frame with a knife.

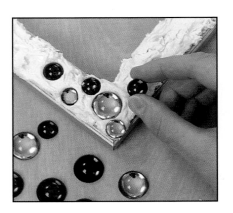

4 Embed the cabochons, sequins or diamanté in the filler whilst it is still soft.

5 Leave to dry and then paint the filler with gold paint.

ARTIFICIAL FLOWER MIRROR FRAME

These mirror frames have been decorated with artificial flowers and leaves, Christmas apples, hearts and plastic fruit decorated with gold spray paint. (Square frames – Juliet Bawden; heart frame – Lucinda Ganderton)

THIS WACKY PROJECT IS MADE BY SIMPLY GLUING SILK FLOWERS ON TO A FRAME. YOU CAN AIM FOR A FAIRLY RESTRAINED EFFECT BY USING TWO COLOURS ONLY AS IN THIS PROJECT, OR MAKE YOUR FRAME AS COLOURFULLY EXOTIC AS YOU DESIRE.

MATERIALS
— AND —
EQUIPMENT

frame with mirror
masking tape
scissors
green acrylic paint
paintbrush
selection of artificial flowers
glue gun

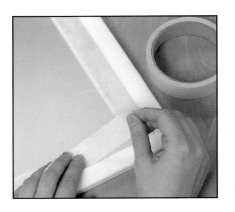

1 Mask off the edges of the mirror with tape, to prevent it from being marked with paint.

2 Paint the frame with one or two coats of green acrylic paint. Leave to dry.

3 Cut the stalks off the flowers and arrange them on the frame until you are happy with the design.

4 Glue the flowers in to position all round the frame until it is completely covered.

Velvet Frame with Appliquéd Cacti

This frame is a mixture of appliqué, collage and embroidery. Much of the work is glued so that it is quick to make, and the stitching is mostly decorative.
(Petra Boase)

 THE ART OF APPLIQUÉ IS TO MIX FABRICS, COLOURS AND TEXTURES TO CREATE AN EXCITING VISUAL WHOLE.

MATERIALS
— AND —
EQUIPMENT

enough velvet to cover the front and sides of the frame

MDF (medium-density fiberboard) frame

pen

scissors

tacking (basting) thread

needle

pencil

paper

selection of fabric scraps

fabric glue

embroidery thread

felt

1 Lay the velvet face down and place the frame in the centre of the fabric. Draw round the outside edges and the central opening. Mark diagonal lines across the opening and cut down the diagonal lines. These triangles will fold back to cover the rebate (rabbet).

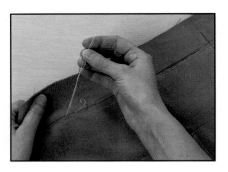

2 Tack (baste) along the marked outline of the frame. The stitches will clearly indicate the outer edges of the frame when you come to decorate the front of the velvet.

3 Draw your cacti designs on paper and then cut them out with scissors to make templates.

4 Cut out the shapes from the fabric scraps and arrange them on the velvet. Stick them in position with fabric glue.

5 Add decorative embroidery to outline and enhance the shapes.

6 Stretch the fabric round the frame, matching the tacking lines to the edges of the frame. Glue the overlap down at the back all round the outside and the inside of the frame.

7 Cut out a piece of felt to fit over the back of the frame and glue it into position, making sure to cover all the unsightly joins at the back.

FRAMES FOR CHILDREN

 THESE INCLUDE UNUSUAL, CHILD-LIKE AND PRETTY IDEAS THAT WILL APPEAL TO A WIDE VARIETY OF CHILDREN OF BOTH SEXES AND ALL AGES. CHILDREN OFTEN FORM VERY INTENSE INTERESTS – EVEN IF THEY ARE NOT ALWAYS LONG-LASTING – AND A FRAME WITH A THEME IS A REALLY GOOD WAY TO SHOW YOU WANT TO CONTRIBUTE TO THEIR INTEREST, ESPECIALLY IF THE FRAME CAN BE USED TO DISPLAY A TREASURED POSSESSION.

MOST OF THESE FRAMES ARE QUICKLY, EASILY AND CHEAPLY MADE, SO YOU CAN RESPOND TO A NEW ENTHUSIASM IN TIME FOR AN IMMINENT BIRTHDAY. OR YOU CAN USE THEM TO ADD AN EXTRA-SPECIAL AND ORIGINAL FINISHING TOUCH TO A CHILD'S BEDROOM SCHEME. THERE IS SOMETHING TO PLEASE EVERYONE.

*Above: a wooden frame decorated with
wooden cut-out shapes of an octopus,
shells and star fish. The decorations are
stuck on with wood glue and decorated
by painting. A fun element are the
moving eyes on the octopus which
make the frame particularly suitable
for children. (Lisa Gilchrist)*

*Above: a frame with a secret. Frames
with doors can hide nice surprises. This
one is decorated with a design of stars,
triangles and small brass discs.
A cockerel in relief guards the entrance
to the doors which are held in place
with very fine brass hinges and screws.
(Jill and David Hancock)*

*Right: a good present for a child – a
frame connected with a favourite
pastime or hobby. The one in the
background is for budding entomologists.
(Bombay Duck) The frame in the
foreground is decorated with a carved
cricket bat, stumps and cap.
(Tessa Fantoni)*

Right: a wacky-shaped papier-mâché mirror frame decorated with brightly coloured acrylic paints.
(Anne-Marie Cadman)

Above: at the top a brightly coloured frame is decorated with all those left-over pieces from board games, toys from crackers and old pieces from jig saws. Below: a pine frame with wooden stars and beads stuck round it. A simple project for a child to make on a rainy day. (Juliet Moxley)

Papier-Mâché Frame with Bows

THIS CHARMING FRAME IS VERY PRETTY AND
WOULD MAKE A LOVELY PRESENT. IT IS EASILY
ADAPTED TO SUIT ANY BEDROOM COLOUR SCHEME.

MATERIALS
AND
EQUIPMENT

cutting mat

craft knife

cardboard

ruler

wallpaper paste

paintbrush

newspaper

scissors

PVA (white) glue

acrylic gesso

red, white, green, blue, purple and brown
acrylic paint

sponge

string

matt varnish

1 On a cutting mat, cut a frame and backing square from the cardboard. Mix up the wallpaper paste, paint a layer on to both pieces of cardboard and leave to dry. This prevents the frame from buckling at a later stage.

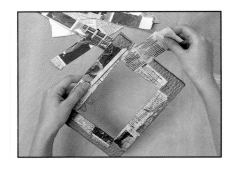

2 Tear the newspaper into short strips. Dip the strips in the paste and wrap them round the frame until it is completely covered. Allow to dry. When the first layer has dried, cover with a second layer of strips.

3 Cut eight 10 × 5 cm (4 × 2 in) strips of newspaper. Cover one side with paste, fold the ends to the centre and pinch the middle to form a bow. Fix smaller, pasted strips round the middle. Leave to dry.

4 Glue the backing square to the back of the frame. Leave the top open to allow for a picture. Stick the bows to the front of the frame and paint the whole thing with a coat of acrylic gesso.

5 Mix pink paint on a saucer from a combination of red and white acrylic, and dip the sponge into it. Dab the excess paint on to a spare piece of paper and then sponge the frame. It doesn't matter if the bows are covered at this stage as they will be painted later.

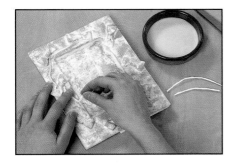

6 Cut strips of string and dip them into the glue. Stick them between the bows. Paint the bows in pastel colours and leave them to dry. Give the whole frame a coat of matt varnish.

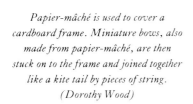

Papier-mâché is used to cover a cardboard frame. Miniature bows, also made from papier-mâché, are then stuck on to the frame and joined together like a kite tail by pieces of string.
(Dorothy Wood)

SUN & STARS FRAME WITH SHUTTERS

An unusual frame with doors. Appropriately the sun is on the outside, opening to reveal the stars in a dark blue sky inside. (Jill and David Hancock)

THIS FRAME HAS SHUTTERS WHICH SHOW A GOLDEN, GLOWING SUN WHEN CLOSED AND A NIGHT SKY WITH TWINKLING STARS WHEN OPEN.

MATERIALS
—— AND ——
EQUIPMENT

6 mm (¼ in) thick birch plywood
measuring 20 × 60 cm (8 × 24 in)

pencil

ruler

clamp or vice (vise)

small saw

hand-drill and bit

fretsaw

sandpaper

wood glue

cloth

white emulsion (latex) paint

paintbrushes

stippling brush

mid-blue, yellow, red, midnight blue,
white and gold acrylic paints

matt acrylic varnish

bradawl (awl)

4 small brass hinges, with screws

small screwdriver

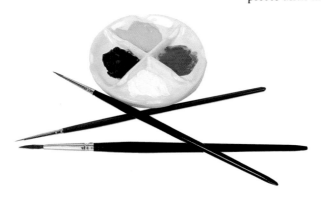

1 On the wood, measure out three 20 × 20 cm (8 × 8 in) squares. Divide one of these in to two. Draw a 2.5 cm (1 in) border inside the second square and a 17 mm (⅝ in) border inside the third. Hold the wood in the clamp or vice (vise) and saw out the three squares. Drill a hole just inside the border of the second two squares and pass the fretsaw blade through the hole. Refasten the blade to the saw and cut out the middle squares. Cut the third square in half. Sand all the pieces until they are smooth.

2 Glue the narrower frame to the back of the wider one and wipe away any excess glue.

3 Give the wood a coat of white emulsion (latex). Paint the fronts of the doors and frame with mid-blue acrylic. Paint the other sides and edges with a yellow/red mixture to give a golden colour. Stipple over the mid-blue paint with midnight blue acrylic.

4 When the stippling is dry, paint stars on the inside of both of the doors with white acrylic paint.

5 Lightly pencil in a sun design on the door fronts and then paint in the details, including decorative brushstrokes round the edges in gold. Use yellow acrylic tinted with varying amounts of red or blue for the sun.

6 Give everything a coat of varnish and leave to dry. Position the door fronts on the frame. Make small holes with a bradawl (awl) on the edges of the frame and the edges of the doors. Line up the holes, attach the small hinges and tighten the screws.

CAT & MOUSE FRAME

THIS IS A WONDERFUL FRAME FOR A CAT-LOVER OR A CHILD. IF YOUR CHILD HAS A PARTICULAR FAVOURITE ANIMAL, YOU COULD CHANGE THE CUT-OUT SHAPES TO SUIT – TRY A BIRD, THE FAMILY DOG OR EVEN A PIG OR A HIPPO.

MATERIALS
—— AND ——
EQUIPMENT

pencil
ruler
small saw
9 × 48 mm (³⁄₁₆ × 3½ in) pine
9 × 20 mm (³⁄₁₆ × ¾ in) pine
fine-grade sandpaper
tracing paper
fretsaw
wood glue
white emulsion (latex) paint
paintbrushes
blue, grey and black acrylic paint
matt varnish
hardboard
panel pins
tack hammer

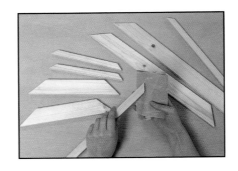

1 Cut two lengths of both widths of pine to 46 cm (18½ in) and two lengths of both widths to 22 cm (9 in). Mark 45-degree mitres at the ends of all the pieces and saw them off. Gently sand any rough edges. Do not be too vigorous as you might alter the angle of the mitres, and the frame will not fit together exactly.

2 Trace the animal templates from page 153 and draw round the cat, cat's tail and two mice on a spare piece of the 48 mm (3½ in) wide pine. Cut them out with the fretsaw.

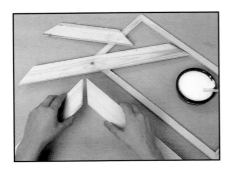

3 Glue the wide lengths of pine into a rectangle and the narrow lengths into another rectangle. Leave them to dry.

4 Paint the whole frame with white emulsion (latex). When dry, sand it smooth.

5 Paint a streaky blue-grey acrylic background coat all over and allow to dry. Sand the frame so the undercoat shows through a little.

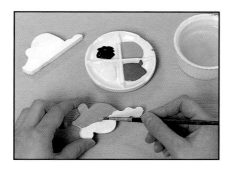

6 Give the animals a coat of white emulsion and leave to dry. Paint them grey and add decorative details. Paint a black mousehole in the bottom left-hand corner of the frame.

7 Glue the animals to the frame and wipe off any excess. Paint the frame with a coat of varnish.

8 Glue the narrow frame centrally to the back of the main frame. This will make a rebate (rabbet) to hold a picture or mirror in place. Make a back for the frame by cutting a piece of hardboard to fit and fix it in place with panel pins.

A smug cat is sitting on top of this wooden frame, waiting for the mouse to climb up the frame and be pounced upon. The frame is made from wood and painted with acrylics. (Jill and David Hancock)

Crocheted Raffia Flower Frame

THIS PRETTY AND UNUSUAL FRAME IS MADE BY CUTTING A HOLE IN THE LID OF A ROUND BOX LID (A CHEESE BOX IS GOOD), AND THEN CROCHETING AROUND IT, CREATING A FLOWER EFFECT.

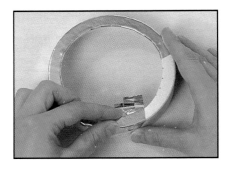

1 Draw round the box lid on to the cardboard and cut out the circle. This is used to hold your picture inside the frame, when completed. On top of the box lid, measure and mark 1 cm (½ in) in from the outer edge. Using the craft knife, score and then carefully cut along this line; remove and discard the inner circle. You now have a frame base. Cover this inside and out with gold or coloured tape.

KEY:

ch	chain
sl st	slip-stitch
dc (sc)	double crochet (single chain)
st	stitch
sts	stitches
htr	half treble
tr	treble
dtr	double treble

2 With blue raffia and the crochet hook, work as follows:

Round 1: Starting about 7.5 cm (3 in) in from the end, work 40 ch. Sl st in first ch to form ring. 1 ch 60 dc (sc) in to ring. Sl st in first dc (sc) at beginning (beg) of round.

Round 2: 1 ch 1 dc (sc) in each of the next 60 sts, sl st in first dc (sc) at beg of round.

Round 3: Work as for round 2.

Round 4: Now work the sides. Crocheting in the back loop *only* of each stitch, 1 ch *1 dc (sc) in each of the next 14 sts, miss the following st. Repeat from * 3 more times. Sl st in first dc (sc) at beg of round.

Round 5: 1 ch 1 dc (sc) for next 54 sts, sl st in first dc (sc) at beg of round. Repeat Round 5 until the crochet sides measure the same depth as the box lid used. Cast off, leaving an end of about 1 m (1 yard).

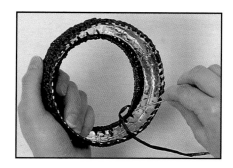

3 Fit the crochet over the frame base, stretching it into position. Thread the needle on to the raffia end attached to the crochet. Over-stitch the crochet to the frame base. Repeat round the inner edge. If the wood or card is thick, use a pair of pliers to pull the needle through.

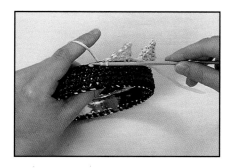

4 Crochet the petals on to the frame as follows: with the wrong side facing you and crocheting along the 4th row from the inner circle of frame, cast on 6 ch. Along this ch work 1 sl st in 2nd ch from hook, 1 htr in next ch, 1 tr in next ch 1 dtr in each of last 2 chs. Join petal to frame with a sl st in the 4th st away from beg of petal.

Turn and work back around the petals as follows: 1 sl st in each of next 5 sts up to point of petal, 2 sl sts in top of petal, 1 sl st in each of next 5 sts down other side of petal to frame, fasten off. Sew in both ends. Working anti-clockwise, crochet the next petal 1 st away from the previous petal. Crochet ten petals round the frame.

Raffia has been used in unusual and creative ways to create these delightful children's frames. The top frame is made by crocheting around a cheese-box lid and adding different-colour crocheted petals. The lower frame has a brightly coloured tassel surround.
(Rachel Howard Marshall)

SPACESHIP FRAME

A FUN, SPACE-AGE FRAME THAT IS SIMPLE TO MAKE OUT OF A VARIETY OF COLOURED CARDBOARDS AND SHINY SWEET (CANDY) WRAPPERS.

A child's frame made from recycled materials: foil, paper, and cardboard. These are used to create three-dimensional shapes which come out of the frame. It could stand on its own or frame a toy rocket. (Rachel Howard Marshall)

MATERIALS
— AND —
EQUIPMENT

pencil

tracing paper

paper

scissors

45 × 35 cm (18 × 14 in) corrugated cardboard

ruler

craft knife

black gloss spray paint

40 × 25 cm (16 × 10 in) thin blue metallic cardboard

glue or double-sided tape

40 × 25 cm (16 × 10 in) thin silver metallic cardboard

selection of sweet (candy) wrappers

40 × 25 cm (16 × 10 in) thin gold glitter cardboard

pinking shears

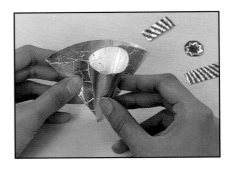

1 Trace the five templates for this project from page 156 and cut out paper templates. Cut out the frame from the corrugated cardboard and spray it with several coats of black gloss paint. Cut the spaceship body and wings from the blue cardboard. Roll the quarter circle in to a cone, stick along the inside edge then fix it on to the centre of the wings. Repeat to make a second spaceship.

2 Draw round the templates and cut out the jet body and wings from the silver cardboard. Roll the body piece to form a cone, and stick along the inside edge. Stick the cone on to the centre of the wings.

3 Decorate the spaceships and jets with sweet (candy) wrappers. Cut out shapes and glue them to the nose, wings and bodies.

4 Cut a star from the gold cardboard, and spirals using pinking shears. Arrange and stick all the shapes around the frame.

TEMPLATES

The templates that appear on this page have been reproduced the same size as is needed for the projects. You can simply trace them, transfer on to paper and cut them out. Templates that appear on a grid need to be enlarged. You can do this by using a grid system or by enlarging them on a photocopier. To enlarge using the grid method, trace the template and its grid lines on to a piece of tracing paper. Following the grid enlargement instructions on the specific template page, draw a larger grid to the correct square size on to another piece of paper. Copy the outline on to the second grid by taking each square individually and drawing the relevant part of the outline in the larger square. Finally, draw over the lines to make sure they are continuous.

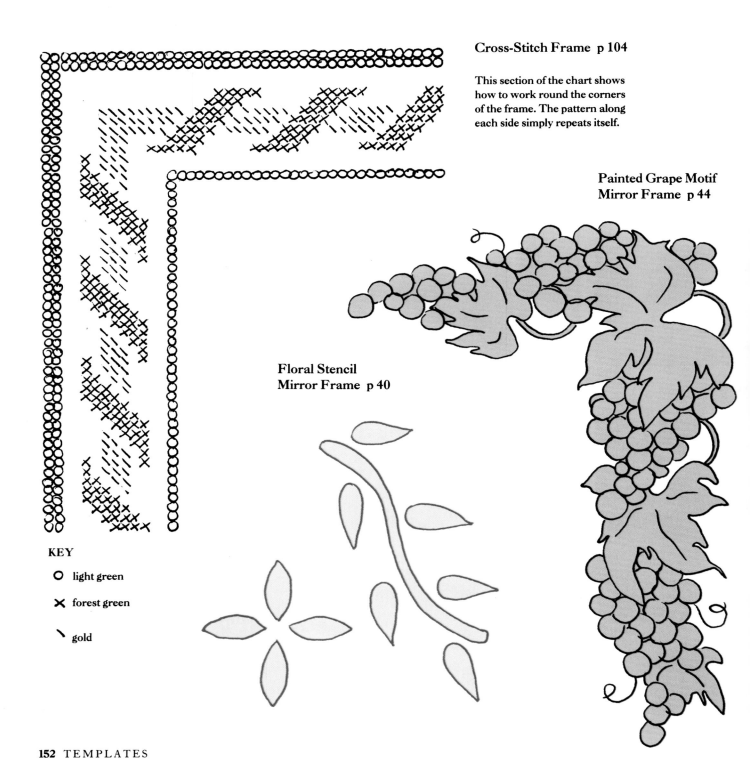

Cross-Stitch Frame p 104

This section of the chart shows how to work round the corners of the frame. The pattern along each side simply repeats itself.

**Painted Grape Motif
Mirror Frame p 44**

**Floral Stencil
Mirror Frame p 40**

KEY

O   light green

✗   forest green

╲   gold

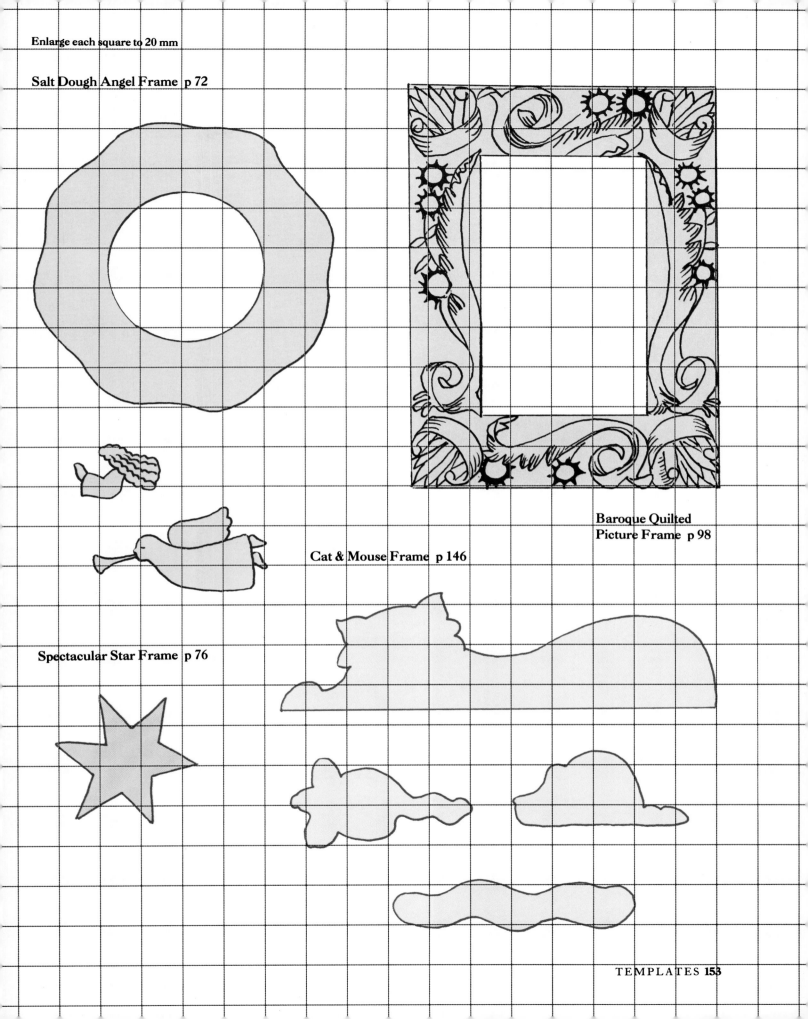

Enlarge each square to 20 mm

Salt Dough Angel Frame p 72

Baroque Quilted
Picture Frame p 98

Cat & Mouse Frame p 146

Spectacular Star Frame p 76

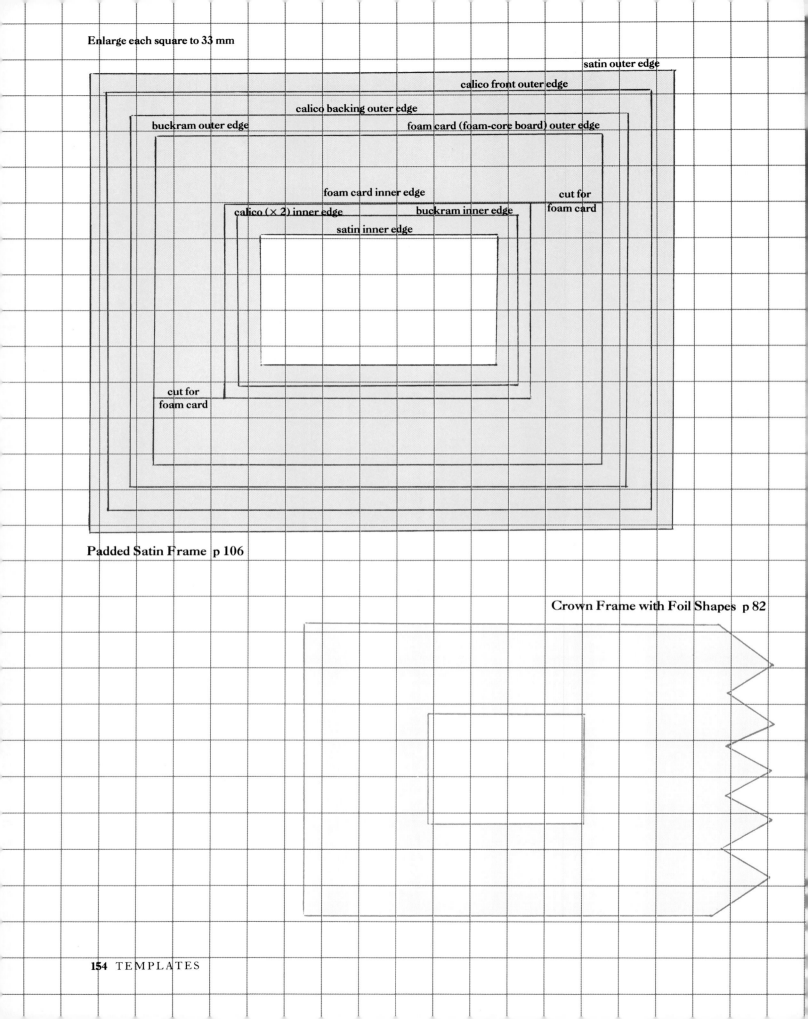

Enlarge each square to 33 mm

satin outer edge

calico front outer edge

calico backing outer edge

buckram outer edge

foam card (foam-core board) outer edge

foam card inner edge

cut for foam card

calico (× 2) inner edge

buckram inner edge

satin inner edge

cut for foam card

Padded Satin Frame p 106

Crown Frame with Foil Shapes p 82

Enlarge each square to 33 mm

Buckram Frame p 100

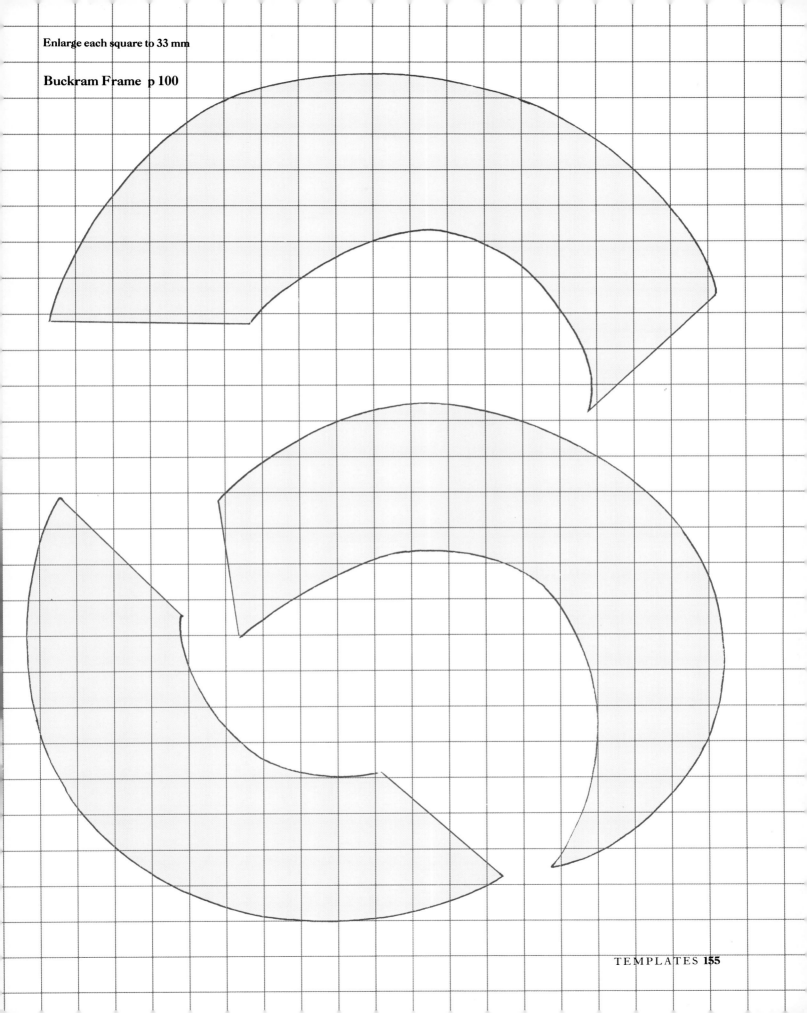

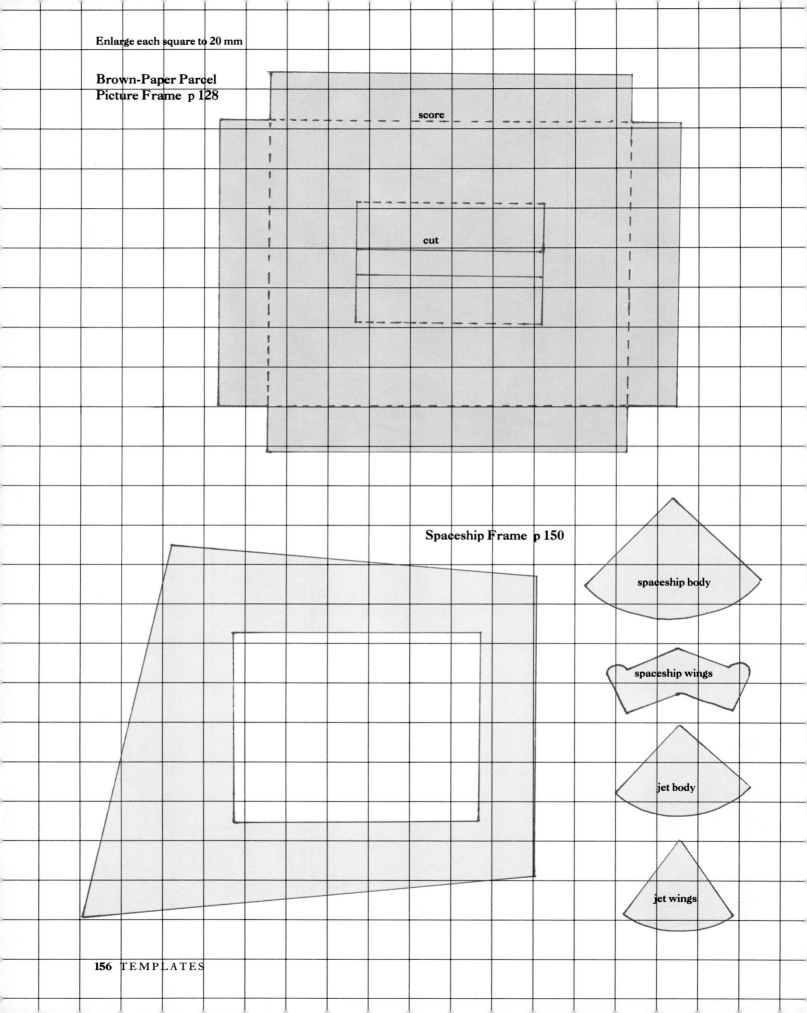

Enlarge each square to 20 mm

**Brown-Paper Parcel
Picture Frame p 128**

score

cut

Spaceship Frame p 150

spaceship body

spaceship wings

jet body

jet wings

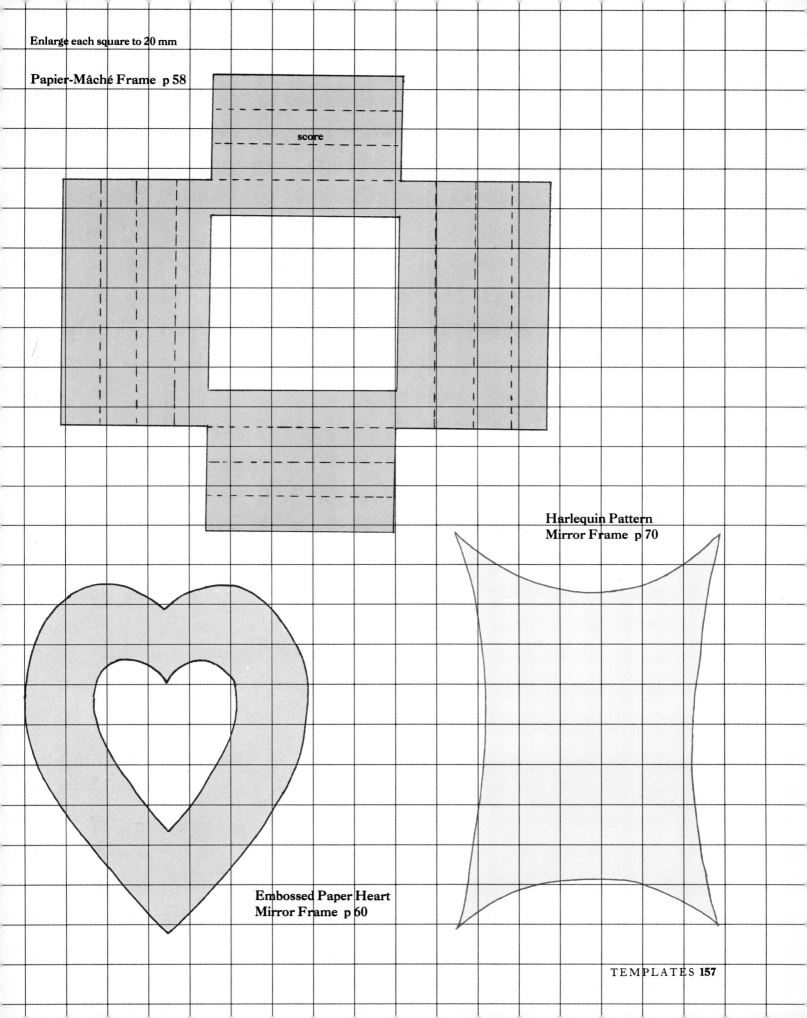

Enlarge each square to 20 mm

Papier-Mâché Frame p 58

score

**Harlequin Pattern
Mirror Frame** p 70

**Embossed Paper Heart
Mirror Frame** p 60

INDEX

ACKNOWLEDGEMENTS

CONTRIBUTORS

The author and publishers would like to thank the following people for projects reproduced within this book:
Ofer Acoo; Deborah Alexander; Michael Ball; Amanda Blunden; Petra Boase; Esther Burt; Gill Clement; Lucinda Ganderton; Louise Gardam; Jill and David Hancock; Rachel Howard Marshall; Terry Moore; Jack Moxley; Oliver Moxley; Sarbjit Natt; Cheryl Owen; Lizzie Reakes; Deborah Schneebeli-Morrell; Debbie Siniska; Isabel Stanley; Karen Triffitt; Josephine Whitfield; Dorothy Wood.

INSPIRATIONAL

The publishers gratefully acknowledge the following individuals and companies who loaned frames for the gallery sections.

Painted Frames
Rebecca Campbell: 401½ Workshops, 401½ Wandsworth Road, London SW8 2JP. Tel: 0171 622 7261
Hermione Carline: 44 Brodrick Road, London SW17. Tel: 0181 672 0081
Lily Curtis: 401½ Workshops, 401½ Wandsworth Road, London SW8 2JP. Tel: 0171 622 7261
James Ellis Stevens: 214A Wellsbach House, Broomhill Road, London SW18 4JQ. Tel: 0181 871 5174

Paper Frames
Hannah Downes: 37A Vardens Road, London SW11 1RQ. Tel: 0171 585 2131
Kirsti Rees: 15 Ranelagh Mansions, New Kings Road, Parsons Green, London.
Matthew Rice: 739 Fulham Road, London SW6 5UL. Tel: 0171 371 9077
Sue Sanders Hand Crafted Collection: 10 Badgers Hill, Virginia Water, Surrey GU25 4SB. Tel: 0134 484 4540

Sculpted Frames
Tim and Karen Buzzard: 106 Broughton Road, Banbury, Oxfordshire OX16 9QQ. Tel: 01295 265727
Jennie Neame: 15 Stanley Buildings, Stanley Passage, London NW1 2TD. Tel: 0171 278 3045
Jo Smith: 56B Highbury Park, London N5 2XG. Tel: 0171 916 2368
Stirling & Bullus: 42 Quernmore Road, London N4 4QP. Tel: 0181 341 3194

Wood, Metal & Glass Frames
Rachel Maidens: 51 Devonshire Drive, North Anston, Nr Sheffield S31 7AN. Tel: 01909 564408
John McKellar: 23 Church Street, Hereford HR1 2LR. Tel: 01432 354460
Helen Musselwhite: 25 Bridge Street, Abingdon, Oxfordshire OX14 3HN. Tel: 01235 528292
Polly Plouviez: Unit W7, Cockpit Workshops, Cockpit Yard, Northington Street, London WC1 2NP. Tel: 0171 916 0155

Fabric Frames
Mark Crowther: Unit 12, Hebble End Works, Hebden Bridge, West Yorkshire HX7 6HJ. Tel: 01422 844808
Rachel McDonnell: Unit 11, Chaucer Court Workshop, Chaucer Street, Nottingham NG1 5LP. Tel: 01159 5842067
Abigail Mill: Studio 10, Muspole Workshops, 25–27 Muspole Street, Norwich NR3 1DJ. Tel: 01603 760955
Lorna Moffat: 38 Canon Woods Way, Kennington, Ashford, Kent TN24 9QY. Tel: 01233 638508
The Mulberry Tree: 120 Hydethorpe Road, Clapham South, London SW12 0JD. Tel: 0181 675 5164
Lizzie Reakes: 68 Oaklands Road, Hanwell, Ealing, London W7 2DU. Tel: 0181 840 7579

Natural Frames
Jason Cleverly: 9A Iliffe Yard, London SE17 3QA. Tel: 0171 703 8517
Tribal Eye: 13 Lewin Road, London SW16 6JZ. Tel: 0181 769 1179

Novelty Frames
Ofer Acoo: 127 Northwold Road, London E5 8RL. Tel: 0181 806 1920
Bombay Duck: Studio 6, 14 Conlan Street, London W10 5AR. Tel: 0181 964 8882
Hannah Downes: see *Paper Frames*
Cleo Mussy: (mirror frame lent by Amanda Hawkins) Unit 72C, Abbey Business Centre, 15–17 Ingate Place, London SW8 3NF. Tel: 0181 785 2433
Sue Sanders: see *Paper Frames*
Rob Turner: Celestial Studio Shop, 17–19 Blackwater Street, East Dulwich, London SE22 8RS. Tel: 0181 693 7977

Frames for Children
Bombay Duck: see *Novelty Frames*

Anne-Marie Cadman: 9 Avon Court, Cressex Close, Binfield, Berkshire RG12. Tel: 01378 290529
Tessa Fantoni: 77 Abbeville Road, London SW4. Tel: 0181 673 1253
Lisa Gilchrist: 44A The Front, Middleton-One-Row, Darlington DL2 1AU. Tel: 01325 332574
Gill and David Hancock: Block 3, Upper Mills Estate, Stonehouse, Gloucestershire GL10 2BJ. Tel: 01453 822488

ACKNOWLEDGEMENTS

The author would like to thank all the contributors; Labeena Ishaque for her assistance; Lucy Tizard and Steve Tanner for their wonderful photographs and Emma Wish for her dedication.

The publishers thank the following suppliers for loaning materials and equipment:

Creative Beadcraft, Denmark Works, Sheecote Dell Road, Beamond End, Nr Amersham, Buckinghamshire HP7 0RX. Tel: 01494 715606
Hobbs & Co Ltd, 88 Blackfriars Road, London SE1 8HA. Tel: 0171 928 1891
D & J Simons & Sons Ltd, 122–150 Hackney Road, London E2 7QL. Tel: 0171 739 3744
Unibond Limited, Henkel Home Improvements & Adhesive Products, Winsford, Cheshire CW7 3QY.

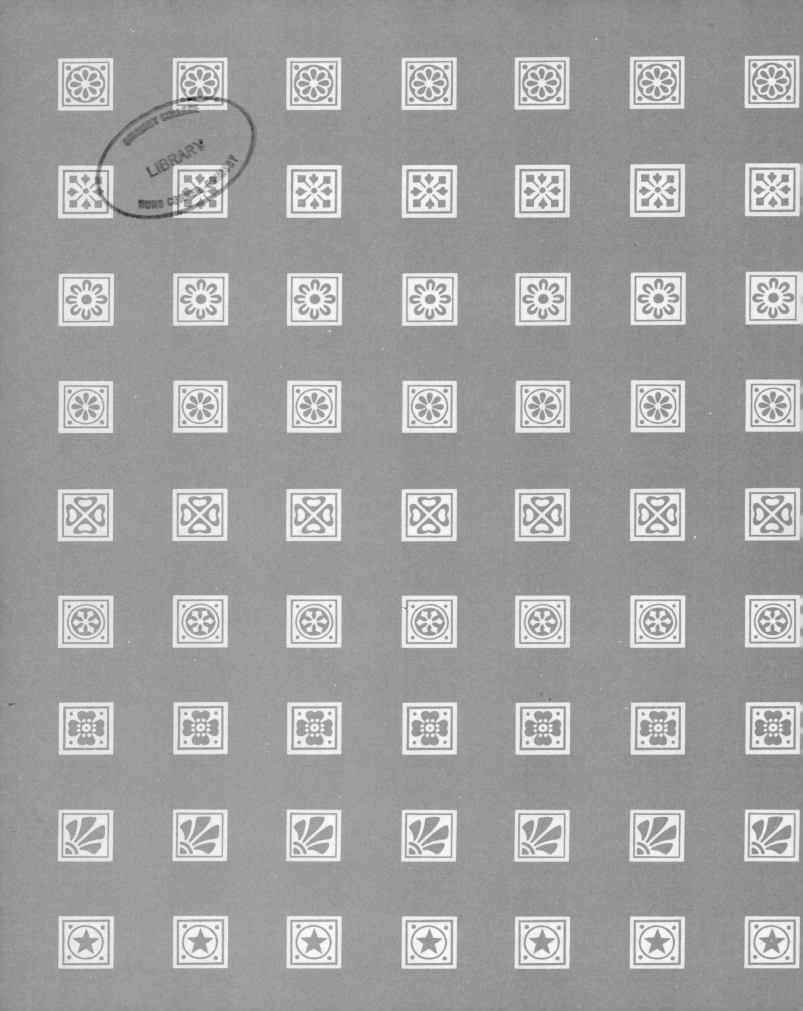